THE Merger
TWO ADAMS - ONE DESTINY

BY RON JONES

Published by Seraph Creative

The Merger: Two Adams – One Destiny 2ⁿᵈ Revision
Copyright © 2018 by Ron Jones.

All rights reserved. No part of this publication may be reproduced by any means,
graphic, electronic, or mechanical, including photocopying, recording, taping or by
any information storage retrieval system without the written permission of the author
except in the case of brief quotations embodied in critical articles and reviews
Scripture quotes marked (NKJV) are taken from the New King James Version.
Copyright 1982 by Thomas Nelson. Used by permission. All rights reserved.

Published by Seraph Creative in 2018
United States / United Kingdom / South Africa / Australia
www.seraphcreative.org
Typesetting/Layout and Cover Design by Feline — www.felinegraphics.com
All rights reserved. No part of this book, artwork included, may be used or reproduced in any matter without the written permission of the publisher.

ISBN 978-0-620-79332-2

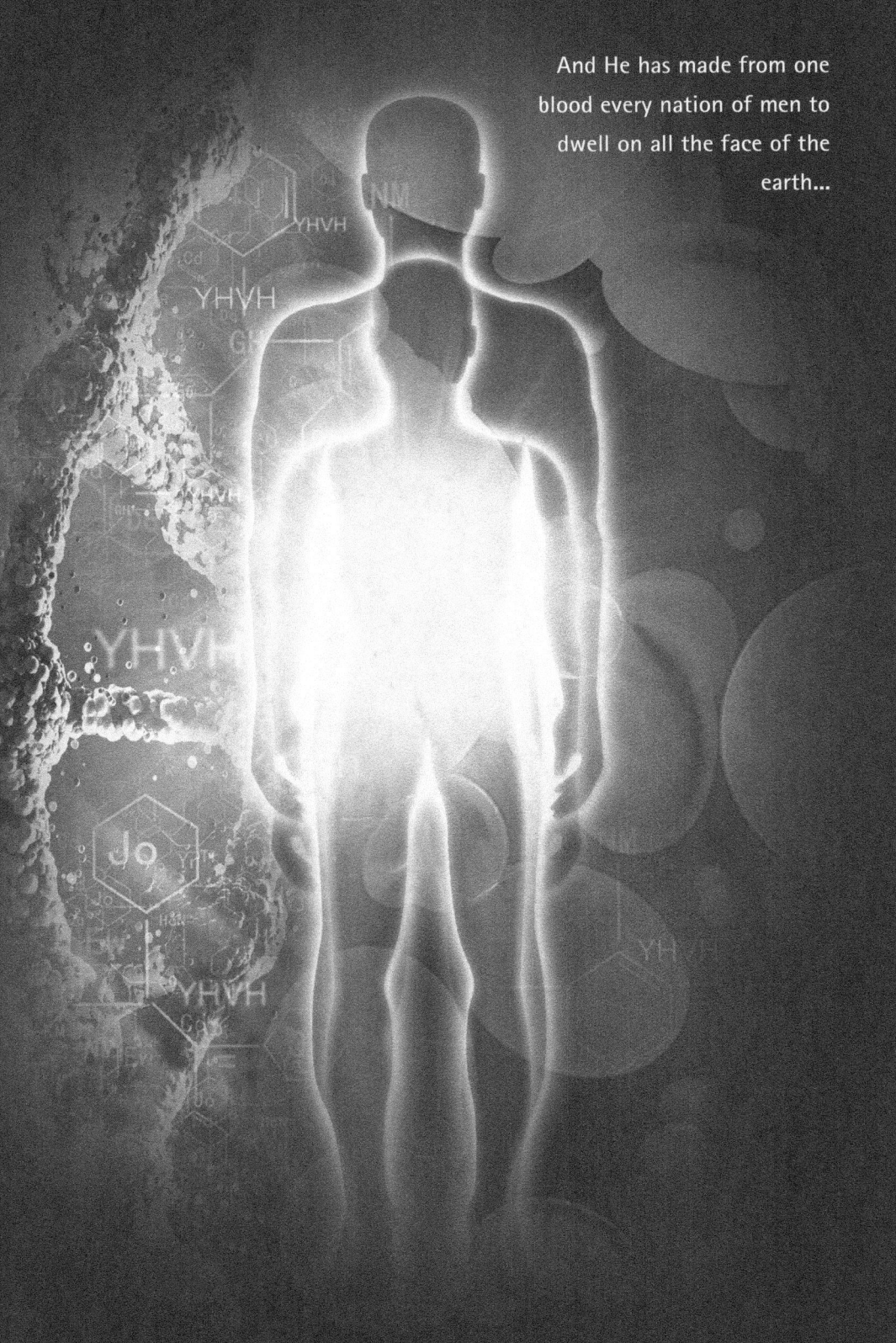

And He has made from one blood every nation of men to dwell on all the face of the earth...

DEDICATION

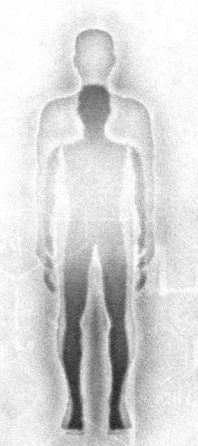

To my wife and best friend for life, Laura...words really cannot express my love and appreciation for you. You are always pushing me to think beyond myself; to think differently, to get out of the box. If ever I've known a pioneer spirit that's ready, willing, and able to head for the high ground of the Kingdom, regardless of the cost — it's you. You have a Deborah, David, and Peter spirit. If God's in it, you're on it. I know it has not been easy, in California, Washington, Arizona, and the United Kingdom. Lot's of movement and not much settling down; I know that was very hard on you. Thank you for all of our God talks over the last several years. Much of what is contained in this book came from years of morning coffee with the Lord and with you. Deep called to deep as we sought the Lord together. Thank you for saying, "Go write, I'll take care of things around here. You need to finish your book!" So much of the time you could have run with your heart's desire, your passion, and your calling. I truly recognize you put much of that on hold for us; for me. I could not have done this without you. I love you my sweet; I am forever thankful for you in my life.

ACKNOWLEDGMENTS

My parents, Gene and Rita Jones. I will begin by thanking two of the most significant people in my life — Mom and Dad. If it weren't for those two people, I would not be alive and if it weren't for my mother specifically, I would not be a believer. I still remember sitting on her lap at the age of 5 when she prayed with me to accept Jesus. Though Dad did not accept the Lord until I was an adult, he never stopped Mom from taking all 6 of us kids to church. She would pack up my older sisters Chris, Loretta, and Candy, my older brother Bob, me, and my little sister Rita every Sunday morning, Sunday evening, and Wednesday evening and take us to church — even after working long hours as a meat wrapper most weekdays and Saturdays. She was tireless in her efforts to ensure her children were going to heaven. She prayed for all of us continually. In their later years, Mom and Dad traveled in a motorhome and sent their tithe to the church I was pastoring - unending love and support. Both Mom and Dad are in heaven now, I can never love or thank them enough for being my parents. We don't get to choose our parents, but I would have if given the choice. I love and miss you both.

Dr. Adonijah O. Ogbonnaya. I would like to thank Dr. "O", my mentor and spiritual father. The first time I heard him teach, I said, "I quit, and I'll never teach again!" His depth of knowledge and insight into the Kingdom, and the Greek and Hebrew scriptures, helped move my evangelical, Western church mindset beyond its place of limited thinking onto a much larger spiritual landscape. I said I quit because I heard him teach, then through a divine appointment only God could orchestrate, he became my spiritual father. I could not be more thankful or honored. When I saw things in scripture I did not have a grid for, I found wisdom and incredible insight in his counsel. While there are times I footnote and reference him in this book, footnotes do not do justice to his contribution to my spiritual journey. Whether through his prayers for me, our personal conversations, his conference teachings, or by spiritual osmosis, he has greatly influenced my thinking and approach to understanding and living in the Kingdom of God — he has greatly impacted my life. He is the person who first revealed the reality of how much God valued and invested in the human body. I am honored he calls me a son. He and his precious wife, Pastor Benedicta, have taken Laura and me into their hearts and into their family, and I can never thank them enough.

Dr. Oral Roberts, Dr. D.G.S. Dhinakaran, Gary Beaton, the founder of Transformation Glory Ministries, Dr. Dan Thompson, and my Chaplain Brother-in-Arms, Dr. Karl Hansen. There are so many people who have spoken into my life over the years to personally encourage me in life, ministry, and friendship. I can only mention a few of their names in the brief space allotted, but I am forever thankful for their significant contributions to my spiritual journey.

Donna Walker and Allison West. I would like to thank Laura's friends of many years, and now my friends, the incomparable Donna Walker and Allison West — sisters! Thank you both for your crazy friendship and the use of your homes to write this book — there is nothing like writing at the beach! The fridge was always full of "Janda's" homemade delights (thank you, Janda!) and the house always open for writing. Special thanks to you, Donna, for all the theological conversations about what I was writing. Our love and thanks to you Donna and Allison, Laura's high school buddies and our present-day musketeers!

Alysia Israel. I would like to thank you, Alysia, for believing in me, and this book. You were the first to contribute financially towards getting it published. Our biggest thanks and our biggest love to you.

Thank you to all my friends throughout the United Kingdom — England, Scotland, Wales, and Northern Ireland — who have listened to me share much of what is in this book. It is great to stay connected with all of you via Skype, Facebook, and our occasional visits!

ACKNOWLEDGMENTS

I could name you, but you know who you are; too many to mention. Laura and I love you very much. We cannot adequately express our love and appreciation for all of you. You have been a huge part of our journey.

Melanie Hart. I would like to thank you, Melanie, for all the time you spent listening to me talk about what I wanted to share in this book: my thoughts, my reservations, and my "why am I writing this book" moments. You listened patiently and helped bring clarity to my thoughts. After all of that, you spent months reading the manuscript and editing revision after revision as I made changes. All the while, you were an ongoing encouragement to "get the book out." You would finish an edit, then I would get "another download" and add more to what you just finished editing. I would eliminate a chapter entirely and then write a new one. What did you do? You got excited about what I added as you looked for those "pesky little dashes" and then encouraged me even more. So many conversations month after month; your suggestions were invaluable and I could not have completed this work without you. Laura and I had many coffees with you Ms. Melanie. Thank you, Melanie, we love you and are forever grateful for you.

DEFINITION: GENDER-BASED TERMS

Throughout this book, I will use the words *man* and *mankind* as all-inclusive references to humanity. It is in no way intended to alienate any specific gender or to be exclusive to anyone. It is simply the term I have chosen to use to describe humanity. Furthermore, I use the words *son and sonship* as well as the phrase *sons of God*. My use of these words is not specifically assigned to men, it is a positional term used to describe mature believers, male and female, who are in Christ.

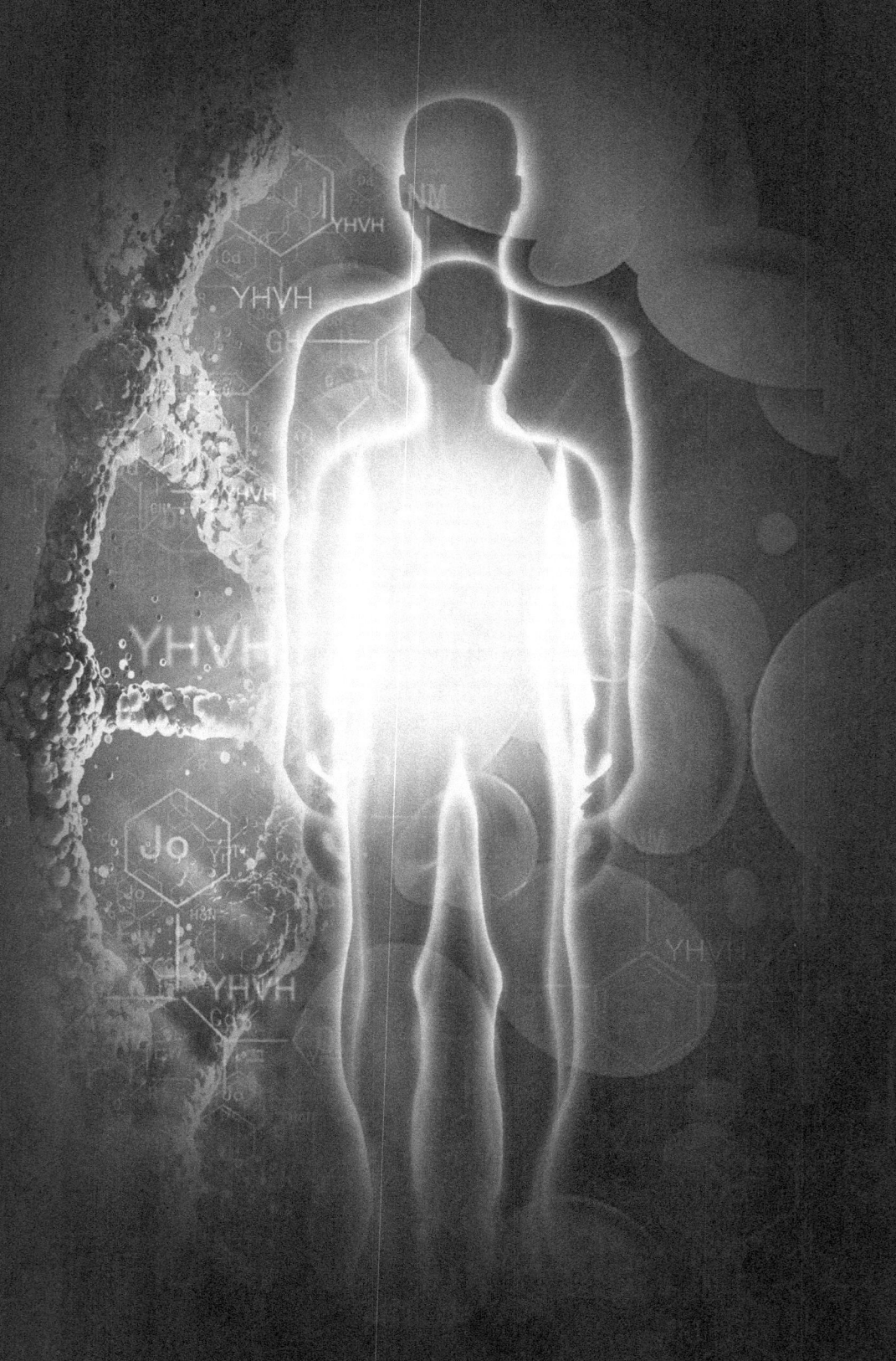

CONTENTS

DEFINITION: GENDER-BASED TERMS		11
FOREWORD		15
ENDORSEMENTS		16
PROLOGUE		19
INTRODUCTION		23
CHAPTER 1:	THE MERGER	33
CHAPTER 2:	TWO ADAMS – ONE DESTINY	39
CHAPTER 3:	HOW CHRIST CAME	59
CHAPTER 4:	WHY CHRIST CAME	67
CHAPTER 5:	THE ORDER OF SACRIFICE	79
CHAPTER 6:	SIN AND DEATH	93
CHAPTER 7:	THE LESSER WORKS	103
CHAPTER 8:	THE GREATER WORKS	117
CHAPTER 9:	OVERCOMING TO REIGN	129
CHAPTER 10:	REDEMPTION – THE BIG PICTURE	147
CHAPTER 11:	THE HEAVENS AND THE EARTH	153
CHAPTER 12:	TIME AND ETERNITY	163
CHAPTER 13:	THY KINGDOM COME	175
CHAPTER 14:	SEEING THE KINGDOM	189
CHAPTER 15:	OPERATING IN THE KINGDOM	205
CHAPTER 16:	REFORMATION AND THE COMING AGE	215
EPILOGUE		225

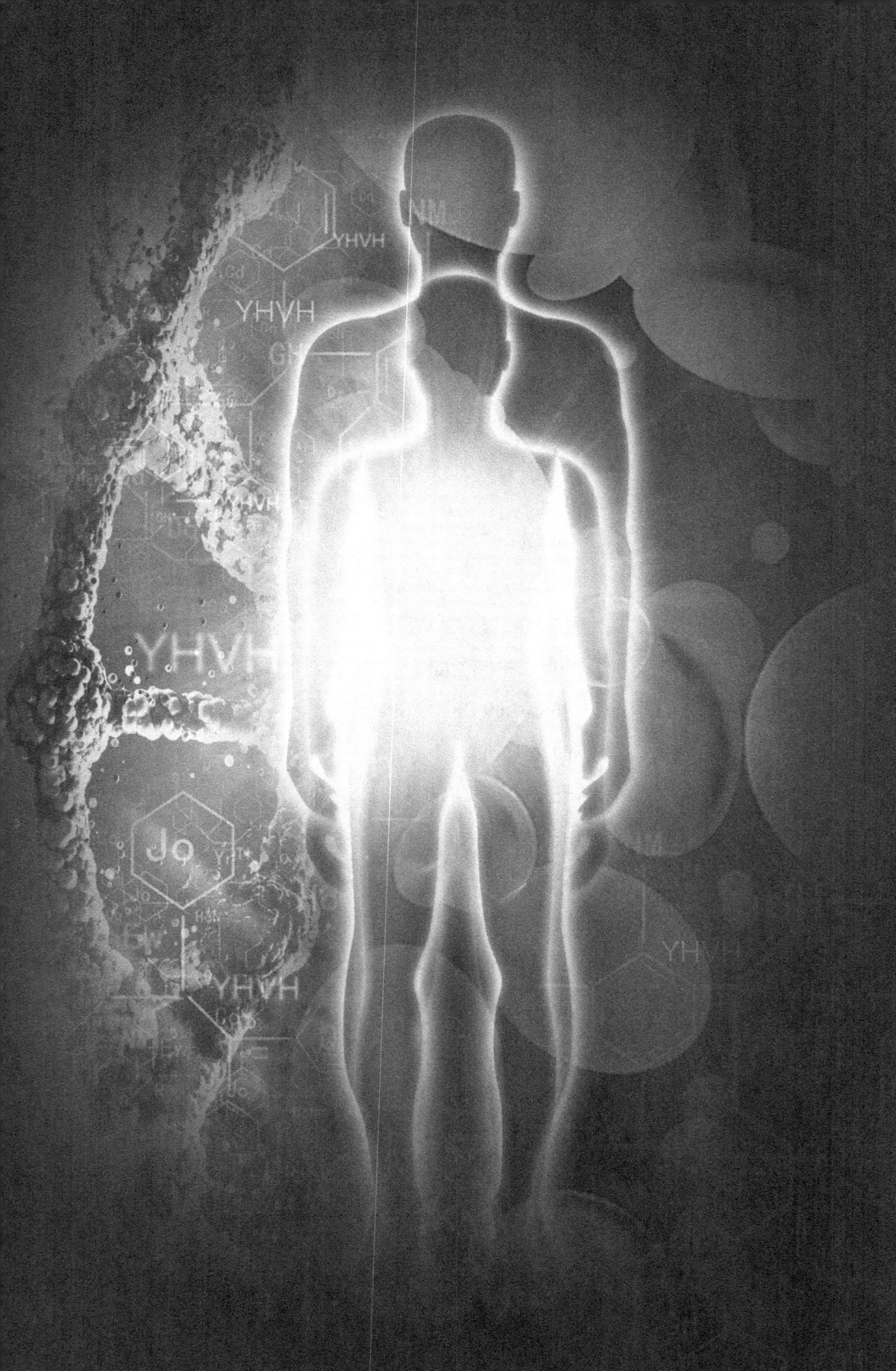

FOREWORD

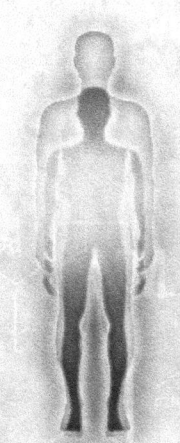

Pastor Ron, as we normally refer to him, is a revelational teacher and carries a great anointing from the Lord Jesus Christ. He has great insight into the nature and destiny of the Sons of God. In this book, he has drawn out revelation that has been hidden in the first and the second Adams. He has provided us, as sons of God, with tools and keys for activating and sustaining our position as sons. This book, "The Merger: Two Adams — One Destiny" is a gold mine of treasures for those desiring a deeper spiritual walk. I know it will bless anyone who reads it. I recommend this book without reserve.

Adonijah Ogbonnaya, PhD

Los Angeles, 2018

ENDORSEMENTS

Having known Ron Jones for over twenty years now, his phenomenal Bible teaching never ceases to amaze me. We have discussed many topics over the years and I consider him to be one of the finest Bible teachers of the Twenty-first Century. Ron has never shied to ask God the hard questions; receive an answer, and then proceed to develop a sound, systematic, reliable, and verifiable teaching based on scriptures. As the study of DNA advances almost daily now, imagine the information that God must have encrypted from even before the beginning (Proverbs 8:22-31). Information that is so specific it would even have to surpass the law of entropy. Enjoy this fascinating work and watch for science to catch up.

Dr. Karl Hansen, D.D.

Ron Jones is "a true Friend of God" and he walks in a revelatory realm that can only come from a deep and intimate walk with Jesus. As you read "The Merger: Two Adams – One Destiny" I believe you will find it to be one of the most profound and inspiring books of our time. In this literary treasure, Ron will take you on an incredible journey of discovery into the heart of God and His exquisite plan of redemption. As Ron carefully unlocks the mysteries of the scriptures in a way never presented before, I believe "The Merger" will transform your life and help bring you into full maturity as manifest Sons of God.

Gary Beaton
Founder - Transformation Glory Ministries
TransformationGloryMinistries.org

I'm very happy and pleased to be asked to endorse this great work of Ron Jones. This is a subject (more than just a subject) that needs to be addressed in these last days. Since major religious moves of God in the past buried such needful and insightful revelations, we need to revisit some of these foundational truths.

I have known Ron for many years and have seen a man that is truly in love with God and not afraid to walk a different beat to a different drum. He wants more than anything to see the body of Christ rise to its intended glory. This book has been in his heart for a long time, but needed some finishing touches of the Holy Spirit to bring it out. One should read it slowly enough to grasp what is being taught. If your mind runs along traditional thought, you will entertain some amount of confusion and miss the beautiful veins of truth. You should also read it with the Bible next to you. Use it as a study guide, not a novel. You don't have to finish it quickly just to conquer the book. Stop after every chapter and think about what you just read.

Some may find it odd to talk about the DNA of the first and Last Adam, but even science tells us that in the human DNA, there is no reason for sickness or death. Something happened in the fall of man to open him to corruption. Christ reversed that curse, but Christians keep following the same DNA strands through the ignorance of their hearts. The human heart ignited by faith in God's true plan and desire (His Word) is the most powerful force there is. Determine that your life will change as you read and study this book — and it will! Yes, I endorse this book whole-heartedly. Thank you, Ron and Laura for your tireless work in God's Kingdom.

Dan Thompson, PhD
Pastor of Faith Builders Family Church

PROLOGUE

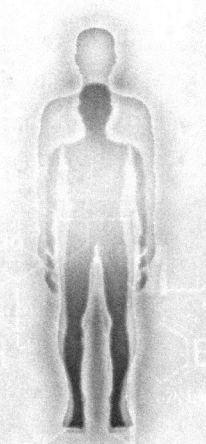

The history of creation is the story of two Adams: their destinies, their actions, their blood, and their DNA. Those two Adams are: *the first Adam*, through whom sin and death entered the creation, and *the Last Adam, Jesus*, through whom redemption entered the creation. They were two Adams with one destiny. God started with an Adam and God said, *"it is finished"* through an Adam. The Last Adam succeeded whereas the first Adam failed.

The life of Christ is an absolute reversal of the fall of the first Adam. It is the story of the full redemption of humanity and the whole of creation within time. The redemptive actions of the Last Adam supersede the sin-leading-to-death actions of the first Adam. As Christians, we tend to view the redemptive work of Christ as primarily spiritual with minimal impact on the present-day physical creation. Since Adam was formed from the creation, he was connected to it; when Adam fell, so did the creation. We need to understand that as it went with Adam, so it went with the creation. Additionally, we need to also understand that as it goes with the Last Adam, so it goes with believing humanity and the sphere of creation they have dominion over.

The creation is awaiting the manifestation of the sons of God so it can reveal its restored beauty through deliverance from the bondage of corruption. *The creation takes on the nature of those having dominion over it; it will always be subordinate to humanity.* When humanity rises to its potential, the creation will rise as well. When we reveal the image of Christ the Son, the creation will manifest its full potential for us in response to the image of sonship revealed through us: "For the earnest expectation of the creation eagerly awaits for the revealing of the sons of God. For the creation was subjected to futility, not willingly, but because of Him who subjected it in hope; because the creation itself also will be delivered from the bondage of corruption into the glorious liberty of the children of God" (Romans 8:19-21). Our liberty frees the creation to rise to the level of our liberty — we are connected through our place of dominion.

Instead of understanding the full measure of redemption available now, most Christians apply biblical principles to control our created flesh rather than walking out its redemption through the law of the Spirit of life in Christ, and its targeted impact on the genomic structures within creation.

The first Adam ate of the tree and activated the law of sin and death. His actions brought separation from God and introduced progressive degeneration leading to death to the human genome and the creation. Jesus, the Last Adam, reversed the fall through His full identification with humanity as both the Son of God and the Son of Man. It is imperative we understand this profound truth; *the Word became flesh to redeem flesh.* That is why Jesus said, "I AM the resurrection and the life." Resurrection and life are pointed at the created, formed from the dust, physical body with its genetic structures - the resurrection and the life are pointed at the body of man. That is also why Paul said, "The law of the Spirit of life in Christ has made me free from the law of sin and death" and, "The body of sin has been done away with." God intentionally pointed His redemptive actions at the human body. The fall of man took place in the earth and the redemption of man took place in the earth. *If the fullness of restoration is not available in the earth, then the fall of the first Adam has greater scope and power in the earth than the redemptive work of Jesus.*

We cannot say the fall of the first Adam affected the human genome and the creation, but the redemption of the Last Adam does not. That is saying God invested more authority in the first Adam than He did Jesus. That is also saying Jesus came in the flesh to redeem humanity without including *our flesh* in the redemption He purchased with *His flesh.*

As the Last Adam, Jesus is the full, complete, and glorified expression of restored humanity and the creation; including the human genome and the subordinate genetic structures within creation. We are new creatures in Christ Jesus with a new genetic lineage. The first Adam was the singular expression of mankind; the Last Adam is the singular expression of restored mankind. We choose which Adam we identify with.

INTRODUCTION

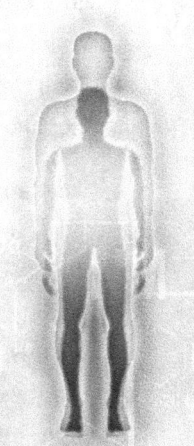

As believers, we are on a journey; a journey to be conformed to the image of Christ through our faith in Him, His Word, and the work of Holy Spirit in and on our lives. Paul said we are transformed by the renewing of our minds. Knowing what man knows does not renew our minds. The traditions of men do not renew our minds. *Knowing what God knows renews our minds from what man knows* (Romans 12:2). What man knows keeps us as we are; what God knows brings about a redemptive transformation. The person of God is the full expression of what He knows. He wants us to know what He knows so we can be transformed by what He knows about us, as He abides in us, and we abide in Him. We should be careful not to engage spiritual processes solely with the mind of man, with human intellect. Paul made it clear: everything we do must be according to Christ and not according to the traditions of men or the principles of the world.

> Beware lest anyone cheat you through philosophy and empty deceit, according to the tradition of men, according to the basic principles of the world, and not according to Christ.
> Colossians 2:8

I have learned so much from those who are beyond my place of spiritual understanding and I cannot thank them enough for their contribution to my spiritual journey. They have helped me understand who I am in Christ. But the truth is, I cannot rely on them for everything I am to know and grow into. God must be my primary source while others help me along the way. God has given each of us the ability to see and know beyond the limited intellect and experiences of man into the limitless mind of God.

Like many of you, I have prayed out mysteries according to 1 Corinthians 14:2. As a result, I have come to understand many things that have broadened the horizons of what is possible in God and what redemption can really mean for those of us who believe. With so many denominations and belief systems (all revolving around Christ), how do I know who and what is right? That is why God sent Holy Spirit to teach us and to take us where no man can take us – *into Christ*. The anointing teaches us to abide in Christ and to engage all that is in Him.

> But the anointing which you have received from Him abides in you, and you do not need that anyone teach you; but as the same anointing teaches you concerning all things, and is true, and is not a lie, and just as it has taught you, you will abide in Him.
> 1 John 2:27

With that said, I must admit that I feel like I live in a place of ongoing illuminated ignorance. I think we have all heard it said, "The more we come to know, the more we realize how much we do not know." We can never claim to know it all or that we have reached the pinnacle of understanding. No matter how much we think we know God and have things figured out, we have not scratched the surface of who God is *and who He recreated us to be.* We love God and want to please Him, but our view of Him is so limited. That is the case with me, and I am sure with you as well. The key is to keep moving forward on this journey – with the anointing that teaches us – into the full expression of who God created and recreated us to be in and through Christ.

I have chosen to write from a primarily Western evangelical perspective. I believe evangelicals and charismatic Christians alike will grow from what is written here. Evangelicals will see there is more to the Christian faith and redemption available to us

INTRODUCTION

now than merely living by biblical principles until Jesus comes. Charismatic Christians will have a Christ-centered scriptural basis for many of their beliefs and spiritual experiences. What I write may validate some experiences while invalidating others. No matter what our spiritual journey holds, *it must always be Christ-centered.*

As first-world, Western Christians, we tend to interpret scripture from an intellectual perspective leading to mental ascent rather than a place of spiritual being. We are destined to become the living expression of what God reveals to us in our quest to be Christ-like. We were created to be the essence and expression of our thought life. *"As he thinks in his heart, so is he"* (Proverbs 23:7). *"Be not conformed to this world but be transformed by the renewing of your mind"* (Romans 12:2). Everyone loves to quote Romans 12:2, but the question is, "Transformed from what, into what?" It is one thing to know we are to be transformed; it is another thing entirely to know the focus of that transformation. We are being transformed into the living revelation of Christ that God has called and recreated us to be.

Christianity is an ever-expanding spiritual experience and exploration of Christ and all that is in Him. It is more than a faith-based revelation that God exists and wants a relationship with us through Jesus. Evangelicals love modeling a life based on "biblical principles" that focus almost exclusively on controlling the flesh with those principles. Principles apart from relationships simply become another law to live by. We cannot relegate scripture to a set of principles to help us control carnal desires in a fallen creation. Likewise, charismatic Christians love hearing and receiving revelatory insight from the scriptures. But if we receive revelation without becoming a living expression of that truth, we have only made ourselves accountable for what we know. We are responsible to work with Holy Spirit to become the on earth, fleshed-out expression of what He reveals to us, and about us, in our spiritual union with Christ in the heavens.

The scriptures are alive; they are to bring understanding and a corresponding life change consistent with the revelation of Christ and the spiritual DNA resident with them. Jesus said, "The words that I speak to you are spirit, and they are life" (John 6:63). His words are spirit and they are life; as such, they should resonate throughout our entire being to transform us into His image. God created us to be so much more than we realize. Once we realize it, we can become all He created and recreated us to be through His redemptive work on the cross, His resurrection, and His ascension.

I find it interesting that we can believe God created everything and then limit God by saying what He will and will not do, and what He can and cannot do today. We preach the sovereignty of God and then limit God as if that sovereignty does not exist. We say He can do anything because He is sovereign, then limit that sovereignty by telling everyone He is not doing "that" anymore, if whatever "that" is disagrees with our dispensational doctrine. We claim sovereignty when we need it to fit our doctrinal views and then ignore it when something happens that does not line up with those same doctrinal views. We are all in some way guilty of engaging in the practice of "selective sovereignty."

We believe God created mankind in His image, then think like we are not supposed to look or act like Him until the return of Christ. What we are really saying is we must wait on a future dispensation of time to walk in the reality of the redemption purchased in a previous dispensation of time. It leaves us trapped in the middle looking back at the cross and forward to the return of Christ. We wait on time to manifest the reality of the already available eternal truths of the finished work of Christ. Dispensationalists put the time in charge of God.

If someone does demonstrate a valid supernatural relationship with God, or has spiritual experiences beyond our basic understanding and application of biblical principles in life, they are accused of being deceived, operating in witchcraft, or working lying signs and wonders. We say spiritual experiences that cannot be readily defined or explained by our intellect and/or current understanding of scripture are, "extra-biblical." We say the gifts passed away as if the gifts of the Spirit and their expiration date or biblical shelf life are subject to our dispensational views. God gave the gifts; therefore, we have no authority to declare they have ceased based on our dispensational interpretation of scripture. God's ongoing desire to express Himself supernaturally within the creation — through the lives of believers — is not subject to our theology.

The God of the Old Testament worked miracle after miracle for Israel through the prophets. He worked miracle after miracle through Christ, miracle after miracle through the apostles, and miracle after miracle through the ages. How is it, as some suppose, that God has been a miraculous God throughout the ages, but suddenly stopped being a miraculous

INTRODUCTION

God after the Bible was written or after the death of the last original apostle? If we believe that God has gifted and used any one person after the death of the last apostle, we must accept that He is still doing that today for anyone who believes.

We believe. We believe the Son of God became a man born of a virgin, lived a sinless life, worked miracles like the God of the Old Testament, was crucified, buried, resurrected, and ascended to His Father. We believe that we can be saved by faith in Him to live with Him forever. Let's face it, we believe.

After all that believing, we should be careful not to discount the reality of God, who is Spirit, living in man and what that should mean for us now, in the present. We must be careful not to discount the full meaning of what it means to be born from above, what it means to have the mind of Christ, to be filled with God, to be like God, to act like God, and reveal God in the earth like we were created to do in the first place. We cannot relegate everything to the future return of Christ as if nothing applies now. We must know, "God lives in us now!"

> Christianity is not a religion; it is an ever-expanding spiritual experience and relationship that results in our full transformation into the image of Christ. It is a self-paced relationship, a self-paced journey. Some are willing to engage for all that means now. Others believe we must wait until Christ returns; the choice is ours to make.

We cannot believe in the redemptive work of Christ and then limit the reality of that redemption by viewing our spirituality and divine potential through a dispensational lens. A dispensational lens is fashioned to show us what God is and is not doing today according to man's interpretation of scripture in each era, even if God is doing the opposite of our present-day interpretation. While it may be an oversimplification, dispensationalists believe God operates a certain way in one dispensation of time and another way in a subsequent dispensation of time and never the two shall meet.

If we are not careful, we will make Christianity a religion that is available now with truths and redemptive benefits that are not available until later, until we physically die. By saying that, we have made a covenant with death. We have declared death to be the savior and preeminent transformational power in the life of the believer – *death is not our savior!* We have errantly developed a dispensational view of everything as if God is limited by time. *Eternal truths are not bound by a dispensation of time; time is not God's master.* We say God is sovereign and then say God is not doing that today, that dispensation *of time* is over. By saying that, we deny the very sovereignty of God that we claim exists. We do not serve a dispensation of time. We serve God who operates out of eternal truth, who created time, and who is not subject to time. How is it that Enoch walked with God and was no more, all before the cross? Apparently, Enoch did not know he had to wait for Christ's redemptive work on the cross to have relationship with God. Enoch was in the earth and left the state of human existence, as we know it, before Abraham (the father of faith) was even born.

Time is not our master; it is a dimension. It is a dimension we have dominion over. We choose what we do with our time. We are time's master; it is not ours. We have all heard the saying, *"Time waits for no one."* I believe and say the opposite, *"No one of faith waits for time."* Enoch did not wait on time. Abraham did not wait on time. David did not wait on time, and Jesus did not wait on time – *they used time to access eternity.* Time passes moment by moment under heaven, but eternity and all it holds has always existed and has always been available to those in time, regardless of time. We will discuss that in more detail in Chapter 12.

We must engage with the person of God to know what He is thinking and doing now; not what He once thought and did based on dispensational theology. God's thoughts must be the basis of our thoughts. I know God does not change, but He has thoughts about *today* just like He had thoughts about *yesterday*. He is an active living God and He is who we need to engage, moment-by-moment, day-by-day. We have been limited in vision because we endeavor to engage the Kingdom of God with natural eyes to gain a natural understanding of a spiritual environment. We must pursue God from a spiritual place of redemption in Christ, with the mind of Christ, to understand the spiritual nature of the earth and all the realms God created.

There is so much more available in Christ than we have recognized. We have been reunited with God through our spiritual union with Him as new creatures in Christ. It is from that place that everything in the created realm has the opportunity to merge with its invisible, supernatural counterpart. We are to be the visible expression of the invisible God

INTRODUCTION

and His Kingdom today. We are not waiting on another dispensation of time. The writer of Hebrews made that abundantly clear.

> But you have come to Mount Zion and to the city of the living God, the heavenly Jerusalem, to an innumerable company of angels, to the general assembly and church of the firstborn who are registered in heaven, to God the Judge of all, to the spirits of just men made perfect, to Jesus the Mediator of the new covenant, and to the blood of sprinkling that speaks better things than that of Abel.
> Hebrews 12:22-24

It is imperative we see what the writer of Hebrews said in verse 22, *"But you have come..."* The writer did not say you will come, or you might come someday. He said, *"But you have come..."* Since we have already come, we have already merged with everything the author is talking about in this passage of scripture: Mount Zion, the heavenly Jerusalem, an innumerable company of angels, the general assembly and church of the firstborn who are registered in heaven, God the Judge of all, the spirits of just men made perfect, Jesus the Mediator of the new covenant and the blood of sprinkling that speaks better things than that of Abel. We have merged with all that is in heaven to see it, say it, and release it on earth as it is in heaven. *That truth supersedes any dispensation of time.* That is who we are, what we need to believe, and how we are to operate today as members of the body of Christ and the church of the firstborn registered in heaven.

Since we have already come to Mount Zion, we are one with God and with the heavens now. Our problem is that we view everything that exists as separate and distinct because we view ourselves as separate and distinct from others. We live as if heaven and earth are separate and as if God and man are separate. *The separation of all things created was never God's intent.* We view the visible as separate from the invisible when, in fact, the visible is made up of the invisible. You cannot have one without the other. You are a spirit that is invisible and exists in a body that is visible. The writer of Hebrews said: "By faith we understand that the worlds were framed by the word of God, so that the things which are seen were not made of things which are visible" (Hebrews 1:3). Scripture is clear, things which are seen were not, and are not, made of things which are visible.

God is merging everything that was separated at the fall. The cross of Christ was the focal point of a divine reunification of all things separated — seen and unseen. Time is irrelevant to those who believe for it now.

I lived in South Korea in the early 1980's. While there, I visited the demilitarized zone (DMZ) in Panmunjom. The DMZ is a buffer zone that separates North and South Korea. The Japanese once controlled the entire Korean Peninsula. When Japan was defeated in WWII, the United States and Russia divided the peninsula at the 38th Parallel. Everything north of the 38th Parallel became the Democratic People's Republic of Korea. Everything south of the 38th Parallel became the Republic of Korea.

When the Korean Peninsula was divided, so were families, communities, and cultures. They were separated and two different ways of living ensued. I have heard discussions over the years about the potential reunification of North and South Korea. They are one peninsula, but two distinct nations divided and separated by the kingdoms that rule them with communism in the North, and a republic in the South. While there, I watched television programs where separated family members from the north and south were reunited; their joy was indescribable. Many were separated in childhood and reunited as adults.

Can you imagine the family and community joy that would come with the reunification of North and South Korea? Political details aside, it would be incredible. That is exactly what Jesus did on the cross; He reunited what had been separated by the fall. God and man, heaven and earth, time and eternity, the government of heaven and the governments of earth, and the communities of heaven and the communities of earth.

That is what this book is about. It is about the merger of all things because Jesus, the Last Adam, came and fulfilled all the first Adam failed to do. When He did, He effectively merged all things separated by the first Adam's failure. It is about the redemptive potential resident within the spirit, soul, and body of every born from above believer. It is about abiding in the Last Adam, *who is the beginning*, the way all genetic and soul-based humanity was in the first Adam, *at the beginning.*

When we engage the person of God in Christ, we will find we have been reunited with our original purpose as sons of God who live, and move, and have our being in the Son of God Himself — in Christ. It is through our relationship with Him that all other areas will be

INTRODUCTION

opened to us, to be merged through us. We are powerful in God and God is powerful in us. We are the earthen vessels through whom God will release and enact the unification of all created realms in Christ, in the heavens and the earth, now. It is redemption. It is a merger.

CHAPTER 1: THE MERGER

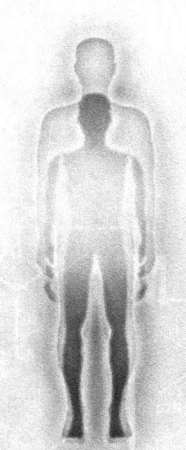

In the beginning, God created. What did He create? He created the heavens and the earth; *the heavens and the earth comprise the created realm.* If we were to discuss the creation of the world with learned Rabbi, we would find a vast difference between rabbinical or Hebraic schools of thought and Western schools of thought regarding the creation of man, and the created realms, but we will stay focused on the Western, evangelical view of creation.

When God created the heavens and the earth, they were unified through the relationship between God and man; God gave mankind dominion over what He created. When Adam fell, the open doors and pathways between available created realms were closed and man was relegated to the earth in his fallen state. Man could no longer move throughout the created realm in his unified relationship with God.

God was not caught off guard by the fall. God did not quit, God did not give up, and God is not starting over or discarding His original plan. He is redeeming who and what was lost: humanity and the fullness of the created realm. It is His intent to return humanity and the creation to a unified state; redeemed and restored to bear the image and ever-increasing likeness of God. Anything less diminishes the eternal value and purpose of the blood of Jesus.

Jesus came as the Last Adam to fulfill the failed destiny of the fallen first Adam and to become the door through which all created realms, once separated, could be merged and reunited. We would be foolish to think the vastness and multiplicity of the created realms and dimensions, from the infinitesimal to the ever-expanding universe, could be perceived solely through our natural, physical senses. If that were the case, we would not know about the atom or about star systems beyond the reach of the naked eye. I also think we would be shocked to discover the vastness of what was in the unified living soul and genomic perceptive ability of pre-fall Adam.

God is merging five things in and through Jesus to bring about the full redemption of not only humanity, but every aspect of the created realm: God and man, the heavens and the earth, time and eternity, the government of heaven and the governments of earth, and the communities of heaven and the communities of earth. Jesus is the Word through which all things created came into being. As a result, Jesus is the door through which all things created will be reunited with their source of being (John 1:1-3; 10:7; Ephesians 1:10).

Let's take a brief look at these five things and view them as the merger of all that was separated at the fall. What is a merger? *A merger is when two things are combined to become one.* I have listed several scriptures that demonstrate this point.

When Jesus, the Son of God became a man, God and man merged to become one: *a merger* (Matthew 16:13; Luke 22:70; John 17:20-21). Jesus brought the Kingdom of God to earth with the intent that the Kingdom of God and the kingdoms of this world be united: *a merger* (Mark 1:14; Matthew 6:10; Revelation 11:15). Humanity exists within time, but God put eternity in the hearts of humanity: *a merger* (Ecclesiastes 3:11). The governments of God and man rested upon the shoulders of Jesus: *a merger* (Isaiah 9:6). After Jesus was tempted, angels from heaven came and ministered to Him and later Moses and Elijah appeared and spoke with Him. The community of heaven partnered with Jesus in the earth: *a merger* (Matthew 4:11; 17:3).

When the Son of God descended from heaven to become Jesus of Nazareth, God enacted the first merger: God and man, and God as a man. Through the restored relationship between God and mankind, the remaining areas will merge to become one again as they

1 : THE MERGER

were created to be.

There were two Adams but only one destiny; hence, the title of this book: *"The Merger: Two Adams – One Destiny."* Although we say there were two Adams, there were more manifestations or expressions of Adam than just two. For instance, there was the singular Adam formed from the dust of the creation. Then there was the pre-fall male Adam after God created the woman. Then there was the post-fall Adam who was the husband of Eve. And then there was Jesus, the Last Adam. That is why the term *"Second Adam"* is not definitive enough. Jesus was not merely the Second Adam; He was the Last Adam in a sequence of different Adamic stages and expressions.

There are times when the term first Adam will suffice because it is not necessary to differentiate between the different expressions of Adam other than between the created Adam who ate of the tree, and Jesus, God's only begotten Son. When necessary, I will identify which Adam I am referring to, either by the context of the passage or by specific reference.

In Paul's letter to the church at Corinth, he spoke specifically of two Adams. The *first Adam*, the one God created and placed in the garden, and the *Last Adam, Jesus*, from heaven, born of Mary.

> "The first man Adam became a living being.
> The Last Adam became a life-giving spirit."
> 1 Corinthians 15:45

The first Adam and the Last Adam had the same exact purpose: to fill the earth with the image and likeness of God. *If you want to know what the Last Adam is going to do, look at what the first Adam was supposed to do.* According to Genesis 1:26, the first Adam was the personification of the image and likeness of God in the creation. "Let us make man in our image and according to our likeness." As the Last Adam, Jesus was the reintroduction of the personification of the image of God within the creation. "He is the image of the invisible God, the firstborn over all creation" (Colossians 1:15). They were both Adams with the same destiny; to bear and reveal the image and likeness of God throughout the creation. As I stated in the prologue, the first Adam was the singular expression of mankind and Jesus is the singular expression of restored mankind; both Adams represent mankind – *we choose which one we identify with*.

Throughout this book, we will compare the first and Last Adams and what it means to and for a world filled with the descendants of the fallen first Adam, and the born from above, new creatures younger siblings of Jesus, the Last Adam — *the Adam who never fell*. We will discuss the systemic implications of the fall on the created realm. We will also discuss the death, burial, and resurrection of Jesus and the resulting level of restoration available to those who believe, receive, and engage for that restoration in this life. "As He is, so are we in this life" (1 John 4:17).

Because we are going to discuss some of the "how God did it" aspects of His plan to restore and merge all things separated at the fall, we need to be open to "how God did it." We cannot be afraid of knowing how God operates in the world He created by His Word. *A revelation from God does not diminish God; it reveals Him and His ways.* In Isaiah 55, God told us to forsake our thoughts and our ways for His thoughts and His ways (Isaiah 55:6-11). We cannot embrace His thoughts or His ways if we do not know them. When we come to know His thoughts and His ways, we will know how He does what He does. With that said, just because we come to know or understand how God did, does, or is going to do something, it does not diminish the miraculous nature of that something. Rather, it serves to conform us to the image of that miraculous something. We must begin with the understanding that God is the Creator of everything, and that everything is designed to reveal and demonstrate His very existence as Creator.

> In the beginning was the Word, and the Word was God, and the Word was with God. He was in the beginning with God. *All things were made through Him, and without Him, nothing was made that was made.*
> John 1:1-3 (emphasis added)

All things were made through Him and without Him nothing was made that was made; you cannot get any clearer than that. *God made everything.* Paul also made this truth abundantly clear in his letter to the Colossians.

1 : THE MERGER

> For by Him all things were created that are in heaven and that are on earth, visible and invisible, whether thrones or dominions or principalities or powers. All things were created through Him and for Him. And He is before all things, and in Him all things consist.
> And He is the head of the body, the church, who is the beginning, the firstborn from the dead, that in all things He may have the preeminence.
> Colossians 1:16–18

Jesus created all things and has preeminence in all things. Any discovery mankind can make is an insight or revelation of Him, His creation and/or creative process, and His willful investment-of-Self in the manifestation of the created world. God is the chief scientist, the chief physicist, the chief physician, the chief geneticist, the chief accountant, the chief judge, the chief author and finisher, and the chief any and everything to do with mankind and the whole of creation. Any field of study is ultimately an effort to understand how God did what God did and how He does what He does within the creation. We cannot be afraid of the scientific journey the world has embraced. Simply stated, the study of nature is a study of the nature of God revealed in nature.

> The study of nature is a study of the nature of God revealed in nature.

I believe God's plan of redemption will have scientific validity and properties the same way humanity and the creation have scientific validity and properties. Why do I believe that? Because, not only is God redeeming the fallen nature of man, He is also redeeming physical humanity and the physical creation. Both are scientifically valid in their existence and have physical properties that can be scientifically verified. God is redeeming and merging the whole of creation separated at the fall, not just the fallen nature of man.

As we look at the redemptive plan of God through Jesus, the Last Adam, I believe we will see the science of redemption the same way we can see the science of creation. When God and man and heaven and earth merge to become one, it will affect the genome of all living things and the whole of creation. Knowing that God's plan is the restoration of all things, let's begin our journey to understand why God sent His Son into the earth *the way He did* and what His miraculous birth, His sinless life, His death, burial, and His resurrection mean to us.

CHAPTER 2:
TWO ADAMS – ONE DESTINY

God did not start over with the Last Adam; He redeemed humanity and the creation through Him. Jesus is called the Last Adam because He is the summation of all Adamic expressions and the reintroduction of God's original plan for humanity.

After God brought woman from Adam's side (she was not called Eve by God, but by Adam after the fall), He blessed them and told them to be fruitful and multiply, and to fill the earth and to subdue it (Genesis 1:28). Though I believe there is much more to being fruitful and multiplying than the mere act of procreation, it is clearly implied as one facet of verse 28. Because of that blessing, *they were the only God-ordained form of human procreation from that point forward.* That is why the genealogies in the Bible trace themselves back to the first Adam; it demonstrates the legitimacy, genetic heritage, and genetic seed line of the Last Adam back to the first Adam. That is also why Genesis 6:9 reports that Noah was perfect in all his generations. It is not referring to the perfection of his walk with God, it is referring to his pure genetic history and lineage reaching back to Adam, he had no foreign DNA in all his generations.

To gain entrance into the creation legally, a person must be a genetic descendant of the first two people with their DNA. That is why it was illegal for the sons of God to join with the daughters of men in Genesis 6. The sons of God were not descendants of Adam with

Adamic DNA; they were not from Adam's genetic lineage. The birth of their progeny was the introduction of foreign DNA that was not sanctioned by God; therefore, it constituted an illegal entrance into the creation. Noah was perfect in his generations and so was Jesus. Jesus had to be the "seed of the woman" with her DNA; *the seed of the woman contains the DNA of the woman* (Genesis 3:15; Galatians 4:4).

The appearance of angels or a visitation from God falls into a different category entirely; temporary appearances in this realm do not constitute taking on lifelong physical form and residence in the earth with a *genetically expressed* God-ordained destiny.

God created the heavens and the earth, and humanity, because His heart's desire was to express Himself visibly through humanity and the creation. God's connection with man was God's connection to the creation: an investment-of-Self in Adam. Humanity and the visible world were specifically designed and created to be multifaceted expressions of our invisible Creator. We cannot view God the way we view ourselves, from a human perspective. We cannot assign the attributes of fallen man to God. He is not bound by our earthly view or mental images of Him. We were created in God's image; we cannot reverse that process to recreate God in our present-day image.

We somehow view God as singular in expression because that is how we view ourselves. We see Him as an individual person with individual expression and individual awareness because that is the nature of our individual existence in a fallen creation. But that is not the case with God; *God is not limited to a singular expression of self.* He is Father, Son, and Holy Spirit with full awareness of each. He is Father God, the Son of God, the Son of Man, the Great Shepherd, the Lamb of God, and our High Priest. These are multiple expressions of the same person. These expressions of God are not God wearing different hats as one singular person; they are *separate but unified* expressions of God Himself. They all express and bear the image of God, as God.

When God created Adam, Adam was a limited expression of God Himself. To some degree, it was God's way of making Adam on earth as He is in heaven. Adam was in unified relationship with God. He was aware of self in relationship with God, but not self-aware as a singular, separate individual apart from God, His presence, His glory, or His image. Adam did not become singularly self-aware apart from God, as we know it, until his eyes were opened at the fall.

2 : TWO ADAMS - ONE DESTINY

It was God's plan for the man and the woman to multiply and to fill the earth from generation to generation until the whole of creation was filled with unified expressions of His image and His likeness. This was to be accomplished through individual beings in unified relationship with God and with each other (Genesis 1:26-28). Mankind was to exercise dominion over all He gave them while bearing His living genetic image and likeness. God would be revealed through unified living souls, as additional expressions of His person, as they remained engaged in an ongoing revelatory relationship with Him to fully mature into all that means.

As we know, they fell before they fulfilled what they were created and blessed to do, and ultimately filled the earth with the image and likeness of fallen humanity, with a fallen genome. God's desire was to fill the earth with expressions of Himself the way heaven is filled with various expressions of Himself. The human act of procreation is the earthly shadow of that heavenly truth. People procreate to break the limitation of a singular expression of self; we call them children. When people procreate, they create an additional genetic expression of self that is born self-aware. Children are born self-aware separate from their parents the way humanity was separated to independent, singular self-awareness at the fall.

God has not called us to be singularly self-aware apart from God, but simply aware of ourselves in Christ as an expression of the God-self He created us to be. Those who understand and walk in this truth are destined to become unified expressions of God to bring *a corporate revelation of Christ beyond our own individual expression of self and the Christ in us*. That is why we are new creatures in spiritual union with Christ and in part, what the gifts of the Spirit are for. They are designed to give us power, authority, and awareness beyond self and back into the heart and mind of God as we mature into a corporate body of unified believers. We were never meant to be disconnected from God, or from one another, through the divisive instrument called independent, singular self-awareness. God created humanity, and subsequently the church, to be a unified community designed to fully express the life, character, nature, image, likeness, and glory of God.

Even though man changed at the fall, *God's plan for humanity and the creation did not*. From the moment mankind fell, God looked forward and never lost sight of the end game: the reintroduction of His expressed image throughout the creation culminating in the full restoration of all things created, including the full and complete restoration of every facet of the original divine architecture of humanity and the creation.

Whether we believe God's initial creation of mankind was as a living soul with a body, or as a three-part being (spirit, soul, and body), we must acknowledge that He created us with bodies that contain DNA. DNA did not suddenly appear and become a part of the human condition at the fall; *DNA was foundational to God's creation.*

All life on earth has a genetic architecture. Plants, animals and every living thing has a genetic structure, a code. However, the human genome and DNA are different than any other. "All flesh is not the same flesh, but there is one kind of flesh of men, another flesh of animals, another of fish, and another of birds" (1 Corinthians 15:39). That scripture details a dominion-based genetic hierarchy of man over every other type of flesh (Genesis 1:26). *Christians must recognize DNA is the fabric of creation and the method God used to encode His unseen immeasurable nature in humanity and the creation.* We cannot be so spiritually minded that we fear the sciences or the study of genetics. John 1:1-3 says, *all things came from Christ and nothing that was created was created apart from Him* — that includes DNA. In fact, I believe DNA is an area where we will see the science of redemption. I further believe DNA can be accessed and reprogrammed by the Word and Spirit of God. The DNA in believing humanity can and will be modified to reflect the reality of the finished work of Christ; *we call it a glorified body.*

Dr. Adonijah O. Ogbonnaya, who is a mentor and spiritual father to me, teaches that the Lamb of God was slain before the foundation of the world and that His blood was shed upon the foundation stone of all creation. Because the blood of the Lamb of God was shed before the manifestation of the created world, no other sacrifice could ever reach the level of trade God made for the physical manifestation of the creation from the unseen to the seen realm.[1] I believe that is an incredible truth. In Jewish Talmudic thought, the foundation stone is the center of creation and the world was woven from that stone. Whether we embrace this Judaic thought or not really does not matter. The truth is, the Lamb of God was slain before the foundations of the world. Months later, I had a dream that confirmed this for me. Dreams are one method God uses to communicate with us as revealed in both Joel 2, and Acts 2.

---

1   www.Aacetv8.com

2 : TWO ADAMS – ONE DESTINY

> And it shall come to pass afterward, that I will pour out My Spirit *on all flesh;* your sons and your daughters shall prophesy, *your old men shall dream dreams,* your young men shall see visions.
> Joel 2:28 (emphasis added)

> But this is what was spoken by the prophet Joel: "And it shall come to pass in the last days, says God, *that I will pour out of My Spirit on all flesh;* your sons and your daughters shall prophesy, your young men shall see visions, *your old men shall dream dreams."*
> Acts 2:16-17 (emphasis added)

God communicates through dreams — dreams are gateways that lead to deeper revelations of what God desires to reveal to us. There are times when dreams need interpretation and times when dreams are self-explanatory. The dream I am about to share is one of those self-explanatory dreams. I was in the United Kingdom with my wife Laura and had been speaking and teaching on some of the things in this book. In the dream, I was outside with a group of people and several angels were also present. The topic of the dream was a film school and film production.

There were about fifty of us gathered and the lead angel started pairing people up for training in film production. The angels looked just like the rest of us. You could not tell they were angels by their appearance, we all just knew who the angels were. We were outside in a park-like setting and there were several rows of chairs set up on the grass. I sat down in the front row and put my arm across the back of the empty chair to my right. I looked back and saw a person sitting directly behind the chair to my right in the row behind me. I knew he was an angel.

While the lead angel was talking to everyone about film production, I turned and asked the angel behind me this question, "The DNA of Christ was in the blood on the foundation stone, wasn't it?" The angel looked at me with a puzzled look on his face and said, "People usually don't ask that question until after they're dead." I responded and said, "I'm very much alive and I'm asking." The angel got up to leave and as he started to disappear into the crowd, he looked over his shoulder at me and said, "Yes." The dream ended.

I believe the eternal blood of Jesus, the Lamb of God slain before the foundations of the world, contained DNA and all created life emanated from and is a variation of that DNA. Humanity is the only creation manifest in the image of God Himself, which means the genome of all humanity was in the blood of Christ on the foundation stone of creation. Every person, every generation, and every aspect of the living created realm was there; *it was the source of all genetic life.* God made every nation of men from *one blood,* the blood of the Lamb that was later in the blood of Adam.

Paul made that clear in his speech on Mars Hill. "God, who made the world and everything in it, since He is Lord of heaven and earth, does not dwell in temples made with hands. Nor is He worshiped with men's hands, as though He needed anything since He gives to all life, breath, and all things. *And He has made from one blood every nation of men to dwell on all the face of the earth* and has determined their pre-appointed times and the boundaries of their dwelling" (Acts 17:24-26, emphasis added). Everyone came from one blood; an original genome — *one blood is a genetic statement.*

Furthermore, Dr. Ogbonnaya teaches that God did not merely create Adam from the dust of the ground, but the dust of the entire creation.[2] As a result, Adam's body was made up of particles from the entire created realm of the heavens and the earth, which connected him to it and gave him dominion over it. His actions on earth were therefore connected to the whole of creation; his actions were universal in nature. After Adam and the creation were manifest from that DNA, Adam fell and the DNA within humanity and the living creation was altered to bear the record of sin and death that entered through the law of sin and death. It was then the process of *degeneration* leading to death began.

I believe when God created Adam, his DNA contained the genetic record of the life and light of God, who is life and light. God encoded a measure of His image and His likeness in that DNA, *the image and likeness of God took on a genetic architecture.* Though Adam did not bear the complete image and likeness of God when created, His DNA was designed to express the image and likeness of God through ongoing relationship with God. DNA is an immense genetic storage device that allowed Adam to grow into the image and ever-increasing likeness of God. When Adam disobeyed God and ate of the tree, it discontinued that relationship and altered his genetic code. That degraded code became the source and

---

2   www.Aactev8.com

record of sin and death that spread to all men through his blood (Romans 5:12). Because Adam was inseparably connected to the creation, the fall was a rewrite of the genetic code in creation as well – *the creation takes on the nature of those who have dominion over it.* That rewrite introduced the law of sin and death to humanity, and to the creation.

I further believe the veil between the seen and unseen realms recognizes the DNA of Christ. It allowed for passage of the creation into the visible realm and it gives passage back into the invisible realm to those who possess it. The veil recognizes the blood of Jesus. The fallen, altered, genetic code is not recognized by the veil. As a result, the fall closed dimensional doors that previously allowed passage between the seen and unseen realms. *Adam's living DNA was his passport throughout the created realm he had been given dominion over.*

The Lamb of God shed His blood on the foundation stone of creation. Cain spilled Abel's blood and the earth opened its mouth to receive it. Jesus spilled His blood on the ground during His crucifixion and Jesus sprinkled His blood upon the mercy seat in heaven. Blood has been involved at every juncture of pre-creation, creation, the fall, and re-creation. The original blood on the foundation stone contained God's DNA, the blood of pre-fall Adam contained God's DNA, Abel's blood contained altered DNA, and Christ's blood contained God's DNA. The living *created realm* is the story of blood and DNA, its introduction throughout the creation, its fall through the first Adam, and its reintroduction and regeneration in and through the Last Adam.

When mankind fell, God removed them from the garden and would not let them return; He did not want them returning to eat of the Tree of Life (Genesis 3:22-23). I believe that deals with more than the fallen nature of man. *If they had eaten of the tree of life, it would have permanently sealed the state of their fallen genome without the possibility of physical redemption.* By not permanently sealing their fallen genetics, God left the human genome an open source code that could later be restored and regenerated through the redemptive work of Christ.

The problem with an open source genome, however, is that man can decipher and edit that code — and he has. That is why Hollywood is infatuated with DNA. Just think of all the movies that contain the thought of genetics, genetic mutation, the genetic evolution of mankind, and the manipulation of human genetics. In fact, the tag line of a recent movie release, *"Assassin's Creed"* reads, *"Your destiny is in your blood."*

Whether we recognize it or not, the world and the current world systems have been built on blood — on fallen DNA. *Every system exploits the fallen genetics of humanity as a revenue stream and means of control. The world is sacrificing your blood and the fallen genetics within it to create wealth.*

This book is not about world systems, but we must recognize the significance of the fall of the human genome and its place in world affairs. For instance, the introduction of sugar-laden products into the world's food supply exacerbates our genetic imperfections. That is just one example. The system targets the genetic imperfections of the masses to cause health problems. If there is a cure for cancer, which I believe there is, its release would be devastating to the world economy. Stated plainly, *fallen genetics have become the platform and fuel for the world's economic engine.*

Health problems feed every system of the world to generate a world economy. The degeneration of the human genome results in the generation of wealth within the systems of this world. If you adversely affect the world's food supply, you adversely affect the human bodies that consume it. Then, doctors prescribe medications created by the pharmaceutical companies to address its effect on the body. But first, the doctors must become doctors. The need for doctors provides economic fuel for the entire education system where perspective physicians are educated and indoctrinated into the system. Indoctrinated you say? Yes, but I am not speaking about an individual physician's personal intent or motivation; I am addressing a global systemic strategy. I am saying as a systemic whole, every world system: government, business, banking, education, arts and entertainment, media, medicine, and agriculture, are mutually entangled to enslave fallen humanity for wealth creation.

It is a vicious cycle of blood-based economic trade. Think about it. The fallen nature of man redirected our attention from relationship with God to dealing with the problems and issues associated with that fallen nature. Every earthly system caters to, and profits from the fallen nature of humanity.

On the surface, governments and other global entities present themselves as the answer to the world's problems. But those systems are not designed to serve or feed people; they feed on people and the weaknesses of the human genome to sustain a world economy. Those operating at a global, behind-the-scenes level, direct their efforts at exploiting the weakness of the human genome to acquire personal wealth and global power. Stated plainly, everything is designed to exploit fallen genetics to direct and control the course of world affairs.

My point in all of this is not to expose supposed hidden agendas, but to point out that since blood and DNA were at the heart of God's creation, *it must be at the heart of His redemptive plan as well or the redemption is incomplete.* If DNA was a part of the fall, it must be a part of the redemption. While we are seated in heavenly places in Christ Jesus spiritually, our genetically constructed bodies are still on earth, under heaven. As a result, we unknowingly live, move and have our being in a system constructed to exploit and take advantage of our fallen genetics. We have been taken captive by the god of this world and locked up in a system that exploits broken DNA. The Last Adam came to set the captives free. Every system has fallen genetics as its blood-based foundation. That is why Jesus came and shed *His blood.* The cross of Christ was more than the redemption of the fallen nature of humanity: *it was also the genetic redemption and born from above, new birth, of believing humanity.*

We know Jesus is a "life-giving spirit" (1 Corinthians 15:45). *But Jesus did not shed His life-giving spirit on the cross.* The life-giving spirit of Jesus did not cleanse us from our sin; the blood in His body did. Jesus shed His blood on the cross, *blood that contained the genome of the created world to redeem the created world and its genome.* Redemption of a world created with DNA, from the blood of the Lamb, is necessarily pointed at what it desires to redeem: *DNA and the life and image of God it was designed to express.* The genome in the blood of Jesus, *in God's new covenant with man,* is the genesis of the genetic redemption of fallen humanity and the fallen creation. That new covenant is activated and enforced by faith in God, and faith in His Word.

Jesus carried the blood from the foundation stone in His body, not from the genetics contributed by Mary, but from the seed that caused Mary to miraculously conceive. When Mary conceived, God reintroduced the *original genome* into the creation to reset the fallen order back to the original foundation and the superior genetic order of the life and light of God. The Kingdom of God cannot be built on a foundation of altered/fallen genetics encoded with the law of sin and death. Fallen genetics do not express the image and likeness of God. God's Kingdom can only be built on the original foundation that is the source of all life in the created realm, the blood of Jesus.

> The redemption must, by necessity, include the restoration of the genetic structures of pre-fall humanity and creation. If it does not, then the fall has greater scope and reach than the redemption. If that is the case, then God intentionally and willfully abandoned us as slaves subject to the prison of a fallen world system. A system built on fallen genetics with the elite and world governments as our wardens. True redemption must redeem all that was lost or it is not truly redemption.

The Last Adam's miraculous birth through Mary was as much about the redemption of the physically created world and the genetics of mankind as it was about the fallen nature of man. John said, "For God so loved the *world (Greek: kosmos)* that He sent His only-begotten Son" (John 3:16). God's heart and vision is to redeem the entire created realm, *the cosmos*. That is why the Son of God left heaven to take up residence in the created realm in a physical body. Now I will probably raise a few eyebrows with this next statement, but I will explain my reasoning in greater detail in the next chapter, so stay with me.

I believe Holy Spirit overshadowed Mary with a male seed (genetic material) that came from pre-fall, pre-sin, first Adam. That seed caused Mary to miraculously conceive resulting in the virgin birth of Jesus. *His birth was the reintroduction of the personification of the image of God through the reintroduction of original genetics.* God did not abandon original, pre-fall genetics; *He reintroduced them.*

This idea presents a possible answer to the age-old question pondered by theologians for centuries: the humanity and divinity of Christ in one person. Most theologians conclude that Jesus was fully God and fully man; I believe that and agree completely. Paul said the fullness of the Godhead was in Him *bodily – bodily includes the human genome* (Colossians 2:9). Even so, our efforts to define that have failed to answer how that could be. I believe His spiritual identity as the Son of God from heaven and His genetic identification with humanity by way of that pre-fall seed provides the answer.

It is important for me to clarify something here. I am not a geneticist or a scientist; I am not educated in either academic discipline. As a result, I am not addressing the molecular structure of the seed from the first Adam. I am not detailing its genetic content or chromosomal makeup; I do not know the construct or inherent frequency of pre-fall genetics. I am simply identifying what I believe to be the source of the seed God used to cause Mary to conceive.

Because the seed that caused Mary to conceive preceded the fall, its genetic structure and DNA was unaffected by the fall. The law of sin and death had no power over pre-fall seed. That seed was the *reintroduction* of the DNA that contained the light and life of God's original image and likeness. Since God is light, the first Adam was created as a physically manifest "light-being" in the image of God. The light and glory that enveloped Adam was lost at the fall, but found and made available to all in the person of Christ.

After the fall and when the fullness of time had come (Galatians 4:4), Holy Spirit overshadowed Mary and caused her to conceive by the genetic seed of pre-fall, first Adam. In so doing, He created the genetic architecture (the physical body) the Son of God left heaven to descend into as the light of the world spiritually, and the light of the world physically through the reintroduction of original DNA. God planned all this so the human genome could be restored into the pre-fall construct of that image, in and through Christ, the Word made flesh.

As we will discuss later, Jesus willfully chose not to manifest the full reality of that light Himself. *That glory was destined for us.* He was the light of the world and we are the light of the world because of Him. "In Him was life and the life was the light of men" (John 1:4). Since God first revealed Himself in and through an Adam, that is also how the image of God must be restored; *in and through an Adam.* God did not break away from the Adamic pattern He started with; *He reintroduced it.* Unless Jesus was born of the first Adam, He could not be the Last Adam to restore humanity to our original place with God, as sons of God.

As Christians, we tend to ignore the physical aspect of the human condition believing God will deal with that later rather than sooner. Perhaps, at the long-awaited catching away of the church. As a result, we somehow think the human soul and/or spirit is God's sole focus and priority when dealing with humanity. In many ways, today's church has become a behavior modification center when it should be a spiritual training center focused on maturing believers into the full manifestation of redeemed sonship. We tend to focus on disciplining the soul with spiritual principles — to control the flesh — rather than walking out its restoration through restored sonship. Believers are not called sons of God because they are led by spiritual or biblical principles; they are called sons of God because they are led by the Spirit of God (Romans 8:14).

When God created Adam, his genetics were an integral part of the manifestation of the image of God through him. His whole being was unified to manifest the image of God, who is light, throughout the creation. Father, Son, and Holy Spirit operate in such a measure of unity that they are one. That is how God created Adam to be: unified in his person to the extent that every part of his being revealed and expressed the image of God contained in the investment of the God-self within his living, genetic structures, and living soul.

Since it was God who gave man a body in the first place, we must recognize that His plan of restoration necessarily includes the body He created. Since genetics were a part of the expression of God in the first Adam, they must be a part of God's redemptive process through the Last Adam so He can be fully revealed through restored, matured and transformed believing humanity. If not, then we cannot physically and genetically bear the image of God the way pre-fall Adam did, and we cannot be fully conformed to the image of His Son as we are predestined to be according to Romans 8:29.

> For whom He foreknew, He also predestined to be conformed to the image of His Son, that He might be the firstborn among many brethren.

We must, in fact, abandon any theology or belief system that falls short of full redemption. If we do not, we are saying the actions of the first Adam and his activation of the process of degeneration leading to death, has greater power than the redeeming actions of the Last Adam and His indwelling resurrection life and Spirit. That cannot be.

> I believe the next move of God is going to be a revelation of the person of Christ. As a result, knowledge about the human condition — spirit, soul and body — will be at the core of that revelation. He was and is the personification of restored and glorified humanity.

2 : TWO ADAMS - ONE DESTINY

Paul said the first Adam was a "type" of Him who was to come. The "Him who was to come" is Jesus. "Nevertheless, death reigned from Adam to Moses, even over those who had not sinned according to the likeness of the transgression of Adam, who is a type of Him who was to come" (Romans 5:14). Before we continue with the Adam for Adam comparison, I will quickly answer what some of you may be wondering. With all the atrocious sins that were committed between Adam and Moses, what transgression did Adam commit that no one else's sin rose to the level of his transgression? The answer: Adam's transgression separated God and man and altered the original living genetic code of humanity and the creation. Adam's sin brought death and a fallen nature to everything and everyone. Everyone between Adam and Moses transgressed because of the genetic and soul-based sin nature they inherited from Adam. Now, back to the Adam for Adam typology.

As we said earlier, 1 Corinthians 15:45 identifies Jesus as the Last Adam. The first Adam was a type of the Last Adam.

> If you want to know what the Last Adam is going to do,
> look at what the first Adam was supposed to do.

The first Adam was supposed to be fruitful, multiply, and fill the earth with the image and ever-increasing likeness of God. That is why Jesus came and why He called us the light of the world. We were predestined to be conformed to His image, the image of God who is light.

The Last Adam is going to do what the first Adam failed to do. Through the law of the Spirit of life in Christ and the incorruptible seed that is the Word of God, He is going to be fruitful and multiply to fill the creation with the image and likeness of God through a family of redeemed and recreated manifest sons of God (Romans 8:14,19; 2 Corinthians 5:17). His birth by the seed of pre-fall Adam positioned Him to be the *firstborn* among many brethren destined to walk in the reality of restored sonship, restored genetics, and restored dominion over this and future created realms.

God did not need His image and likeness in the realm of His pre-creation existence; it was already there. He wanted, and presently wants it, in the created realm. That is why He created Adam in His image in the first place. Christ's sacrifice on the cross was a Son-for-son-exchange and redemptive reversal to restore the image, likeness, and light of God back to man in the created realm where He wants it revealed.

The first Adam was a son of God; therefore, the only sacrifice sufficient to redeem a fallen son of God, is a Son of God. The only comparable sacrifice for an Adam is an Adam. *They were two Adams with one destiny.* They were of the same divine genetic stream, with the same divine purpose and destiny for that stream. They were to fill the earth with the image and ever-increasing likeness of God as they matured to subdue the creation, He gave them dominion over.

We have got to get over our false sense of humility and stop acting like it is honorable to view ourselves as fallen humanity waiting to be restored. For some reason, we feel like we must remain small so God remains big. We do not need to remain small for God to be big; *He is big all by Himself.* Jesus did not come into the earth, live a sinless life, endure the cross and the grave to leave us in a fallen state. It is an indictment against the redemptive work of Christ to think that way. He has deposited in us all that is necessary to bring about our full redemption.

The Word the worlds were made by, became the Word made flesh to redeem our flesh. We are now born of *that* incorruptible seed, *that* Word of God. The Word that created the worlds, the Word that became flesh, and the Word that we are born of are all the same Word – the Word of God. That is *who* abides in us for our complete redemption, now (John 1:1-5, 14, 1 Peter 1:23).

When a seed is planted, it contains the genetic material to become what it is destined to become. So it is with those of us who are born of incorruptible seed that is the Word of God. Jesus did not say, "Hold on, I've got more work to do to ensure your full redemption." Jesus said, "It is finished!" Some may say we are required to wait until we get to heaven to walk in the fullness of redemption. The reality is, we are in heaven. Because God merged God and man, and heaven and earth in Christ, we are seated there in Christ Jesus with complete access to all that is available there.

In a moment, we will discuss the parallel actions of the first and Last Adams. But first, we need to further confirm this Adam-for-Adam, Son-for-son paradigm that we have been talking about. In Romans 5:17, Paul made it clear that it was an Adam-for-Adam comparison involving two specific people, the fallen first Adam, and Jesus Christ, the Last Adam.

2 : TWO ADAMS – ONE DESTINY

> For if by one man's offense (the first Adam – author added) death reigned through the one, much more those who receive abundance of grace and of the gift of righteousness will reign in life through the One, Jesus Christ.
> Romans 5:17

Death entered through the first Adam and redemption through Jesus Christ, the Last Adam. The Last Adam reversed the offense of the first Adam and it is through Him that we are redeemed and restored to our full identity and destiny as sons of God *to reign in life*. Now, let's look at some astounding parallels between the first Adam and Last Adam to make this truth even clearer.

The first Adam was a son of God (Luke 3:38); the Last Adam was a Son of God (Matthew 3:17; 17:5). The first Adam was a man created in the image and likeness of God (Genesis 1:26-27); the Last Adam was God born in the image and likeness of man (Philippians 2:7-8). The first Adam died as a willful act of disobedience (Genesis 2:16; 3:6); the Last Adam died as a willful act of obedience (Philippians 2:8). The first Adam ate of a tree and hid amongst the trees (Genesis 3:6,8); the Last Adam died on a tree. God opened the first Adam's side to create woman (a genetically comparable one) from within him; the Last Adam's side was pierced on the cross. When the first Adam fell, God told him the ground would produce thorns and thistles for him and he would eat bread by the sweat of his brow (Genesis 3:18-19). The Last Adam was the bread of life whose sweat became drops of blood that fell to the ground, and later took those thorns and thistles on His brow (Luke 22:44, John 6:48; 19:5).

Lastly, the first Adam was created from the dust of the creation and he returned to dust. The Last Adam was buried in a tomb and emerged bodily without returning to dust as the resurrection of humanity; *including the human genome.*

These, I believe, are incredible parallels demonstrating an Adam-for-Adam, item-for-item, Son-for-son sacrifice and redemptive reversal. You do not send a servant to redeem a son; you send a Son to redeem a son. It was a Son-for-son, step-by-step reversal to counter the curse at its source to redeem all that was lost by the first Adam. The first Adam embodied the fall of humanity; the Last Adam embodied the restoration of humanity and the entire created realm (Romans 5:12-19). Simply stated,

> Adam ate of the tree and hid amongst the trees,
> So Jesus entered the trees and died on a tree,
> to nail back to the tree, what Adam ate of the tree,
> to bring him back from behind the trees
> and into the presence of God again.

After they ate of the tree, Adam and the woman hid amongst the trees of the garden. God called to them and the Word of God resonated through the trees to the place they were hiding. That was a prophetic demonstration that the Word of God would enter the creation and pass through the very thing they hid behind — trees — to join them. That is exactly what happened. Jesus, the Word of God made flesh, entered the creation, passed through the cross (trees) and descended to bring those who had fallen back into His presence (Ephesians 4:7-10).

While it is true that Jesus died for all of us, His actions and atoning sacrifice were pointed specifically at the first Adam so He could reverse the fall at the very source of its entrance into the creation. His actions had to cover the full landscape of time to redeem those living in various times throughout the full landscape of human existence — beginning with the first Adam. As we will see in Chapter 5, the interaction between God, Cain, and Abel also played a role in how and why Christ would die the way He did.

When God created the first Adam, the genome for the entire human race existed in that one man. All biological humanity that would ever exist would come from the genome resident within the blood of that first body. Stated plainly, we all existed genetically in the blood on the foundation stone that was the source of all life, and we all existed genetically within the blood of the first Adam who was the God-ordained source of all procreated humanity. When God breathed the breath of life into the first Adam, God made us genetically alive together in and with him. We were all one blood; Adam's actions affected his blood and affected us because we were in him genetically (Genesis 2:7; Acts 17:24-26). This same truth is evident with Abraham and Levi also.

2 : TWO ADAMS - ONE DESTINY

> Even Levi, who receives tithes, paid tithes through Abraham, so to speak, for he was still in the loins of his father when Melchizedek met him.
> Hebrews 7:9-10 (emphasis added)

The writer of Hebrews said Levi paid tithes to Melchizedek because he was in the loins — the genome — of Abraham when Abraham gave a tithe to Melchizedek.

When we were born from above, God made us *alive together with Christ* and caused us to be raised up and seated together with Him in heavenly places (Ephesians 2:5-6). We are all now alive and abiding in Christ Jesus, the Last Adam, the way we were genetically alive and abiding in the first Adam. We are all one blood again; the original blood of the Lamb.

Jesus is a life-giving spirit. When we are born from above, we are a new creature; something that never existed before. Even so, our bodies are still on a journey to full restoration. We are on a journey to bear the full image and likeness of God. Though we are new creatures in Christ the Last Adam, our minds are still conformed to this world. By default, we are conformed to the first Adam and the world systems built on and through his altered/fallen genome.

We think and feel from our fallen memories so we continue to bear the genetic image of our fallen experiences. Our DNA still speaks from its reinforced memory of the law of sin and death. But now, we have been born of incorruptible seed that is the Word of God (1 Peter 1:23). If we do not water that seed with faith, it cannot fully germinate to produce the harvest of wholeness within its spiritual and genetic architecture. That is why a revelation of Jesus is so important to the manifestation of our full redemption. When we embrace God's Word and think like redeemed humanity that abides in Christ, wherein all things in heaven and earth are reconciled, we will find ourselves going through a faith-filled transformational process that will enable us to fully and completely bear the image and likeness of God (Romans 12:1-2, Ephesians 1:10). That faith-filled transformational process will affect our DNA to replace the memory and residue of the law of sin and death recorded in the genetic structures of our physical bodies, with the law of the Spirit of life in Christ. We will explain that in greater detail in Chapter 6.

In summary, the history of the creation is the story of two people: the first Adam and the Last Adam, their blood, and the DNA it contained. God began with Adam, the first created son who fell; and He is finishing with Jesus, His only begotten Son; who did not fall. Jesus is the Last Adam from heaven who redeemed humanity and the creation. All living created things emanated from the living DNA in the blood of the Lamb of God shed before the foundations of the world. Adam was created in the image of God and that living DNA was resident within him.

Adam fell and the God DNA that was the source and record of life and light in him was altered to become the genetic source and record of sin and death. Adam's disobedient actions — and the resulting altered genetic code — introduced the law of sin and death to humanity and the creation. That altered DNA, from one blood, was then passed to and through his descendants to populate the earth. As a result, world systems were built and crafted to meet and take advantage of the needs created by the fallen human genome.

When the fullness of time came, Holy Spirit overshadowed Mary and caused her to miraculously conceive by the seed — the genetic material — of pre-fall Adam. That pre-fall, pre-sin seed, contained original God DNA to reintroduce the source and record of life and light in the genome of Jesus, and ultimately, believing humanity. When we are born of incorruptible seed, we are realigned with God's original plan for humanity in Christ through the spiritual *and* genetic reality of His obedient redemptive actions. Our journey must begin with the understanding that we have been empowered by God to walk in the fullness of the redemption found in our kinsmen redeemer, the Last Adam, Jesus.

2 : TWO ADAMS – ONE DESTINY

CHAPTER 3: HOW CHRIST CAME

The Word made flesh. I believe the Word made flesh means the person of our unseen God, who is light, spoke from within Himself to encode His own nature and His own image into DNA. He encoded His image into human DNA to invest and visibly manifest Himself and His glory in the flesh, in His creation (John 1:14).

Jesus called Himself both the Son of God and the Son of Man. While Jesus referred to Himself as the Son of God *five or six times*, He referred to Himself as the Son of Man over *eighty times* throughout the gospels. If you are a son, then you have a father. He is clearly the Son of God because of where He came from *as God, who is Spirit*. I believe He is the Son of Man, the Last Adam, and our kinsmen redeemer because of who His genetic father was. He was truly the Son of God, truly the Son of Man, and truly the Last Adam born in the earth to reverse the actions and consequences of the fallen first Adam.

We emphasized genetics as a part of the first Adam and creation in Chapter 2: "Christians must recognize *DNA is the fabric of creation and the method God used to encode His unseen immeasurable nature in the visible world.*"

> He was in the beginning with God. *All things were made through Him, and without Him, nothing was made that was made.*
> John 1:2-3 (emphasis added)

All things came from and through Christ who is the Word of God. Nothing that was created was created apart from Him, *including DNA*. When the fullness of time came, the Word that was God and created all things, entered the creation to become a part of what He created; He became flesh *with DNA*.

> And the *Word became flesh* and dwelt among us, and we beheld His glory, the glory as of the only-begotten of the Father, full of grace and truth.
> John 1:14 (emphasis added)

Jesus, the Son of God; *Jesus*, the Word of God; *Jesus*, the only-begotten of the Father; *Jesus*, who was in heaven in the form of God, descended into the earth and became flesh. Why did He become flesh? He had to become one with every aspect of human existence to redeem and elevate every aspect of human existence. He had to become flesh to redeem flesh and He had to become Adam to redeem Adam and his fallen descendants. *The Word that created the world became flesh to redeem the world He created.*

It is important to note that while scripture tells us the Word was God and the Word was with God and the Word that was God became flesh, *it does not specify the source of the flesh He became* (John 1:14). The scriptures do make it clear, however, that Jesus, God's Son, left heaven to appear as a man.

> Let this mind be in you which was also in Christ Jesus, *who, being in the form of God*, did not consider it robbery to be equal with God,
> but made Himself of no reputation,
> *taking the form of a bondservant, and coming in the likeness of men.*
> *And being found in appearance as a man*, He humbled Himself and became obedient to the point of death, even the death of the cross.
> Philippians 2:5-8 (emphasis added)

We know Jesus was in the form of God and that He left heaven and descended into the earth to take on the form of a bondservant, to come in the likeness of men, and to become flesh. But since the scriptures do not specify the source of the flesh He became, we should start with what we do know. *We know the Son of God left heaven to become flesh and we know Mary conceived and gave birth to Him as the Son of Man, the Word made flesh.*

> Therefore, the Lord Himself will give you a sign: Behold the virgin *shall conceive* and bear a Son, and shall call His name Immanuel.
> Isaiah 7:14 (emphasis added)

> And behold, *you will conceive in your womb* and bring forth a Son, and shall call His name Jesus.
> Luke 1:31 (emphasis added)

> And when eight days were completed for the circumcision of the Child, His name was called Jesus, the name given by the angel *before He was conceived in the womb.*
> Luke 2:21 (emphasis added)

From these scriptures, it is very clear that Mary *conceived*. Why is it important to know Mary conceived? Because Mary was not a surrogate mother. A male body did not descend from heaven to take up residence in her womb. Mary was a contributing factor in Christ's transition from heaven into the Word made flesh, form of man, in the earth. To conceive means a male seed miraculously entered the reproductive region of her body as a part of the procreative process God established and ordained when He created mankind.

> Then God blessed them, *and God said to them, "Be fruitful and multiply;* fill the earth and subdue it; have dominion over the fish of the sea, over the birds of the air, and over every living thing that moves on the earth."
> Genesis 1:28 (emphasis added)

When Mary conceived, she made a *genetic contribution* to the Word of God becoming flesh. If she did not, then God violated the procreative order He established in Genesis. Also, and equally as important, her genetic contribution was the fulfillment of scripture that made Jesus the "*seed of the woman*" (Genesis 3:15). If Mary's seed was not involved, then Jesus was not the seed of the woman. Furthermore, Mary's genetic contribution also fulfilled the prophetic word that Jesus would be a descendant of David (Luke 3:23-38). If Mary did not *actually conceive*, then her seed was not involved and Jesus was not a descendant of David. It is evident that Jesus was born *of a woman*, not merely *through a woman*. If He was not, then all prophetic scriptures declaring a virgin would *conceive* were not fulfilled through Mary and He would not be *born of a woman* under the law.

> When the fullness of time had come,
> God sent forth His Son *born of a woman*, born under the law.
> Galatians 4:4 (emphasis added)

Since we know Mary conceived, the question is: "What process did God use to facilitate His Son, the Word of God, becoming the Son of Man and the Word made flesh, to take on the form of a bondservant? The answer? Holy Spirit overshadowed Mary to miraculously introduce the pre-fall, pre-sin seed of the first Adam to cause her to conceive.

The next logical question is, "If the seed came from the first Adam, why is He called the Son of God?" The angel told Mary that Holy Spirit would come upon her and the power of the Most High would overshadow her, *for that reason* He would be called the Son of God (Luke 1:35). In the context of that scripture, Jesus was not called the Son of God because of the source or origin of the seed itself. He was called the Son of God because of Holy Spirit's involvement in the miraculous conception; man was not involved. Holy Spirit introduced the pre-fall seed of Adam that caused Mary to conceive.

I spent several years in both Bible College and university studying theology where my education was entirely focused on biblical studies and ministry. In all the years I studied, every institution emphasized that the sin nature is passed on through the male and that is why Jesus could be born of Mary and not have a sin nature; no man with a sin nature was His father. While I do believe that, I submit that is a stand-alone, time-based answer given by those living inside of time with a linear time-based paradigm. *God is not restricted by time.*

We assume that since there was no sinless man in the earth when the fullness of time had come, that no man *on or from the earth* could be His father. Even if there had been a sinless man at the time, procreating with a sinless man would have nullified Christ's virgin birth. We further assume that since He is called the Son of God, that God is His genetic Father through the miraculous appearance of a *heavenly* male seed that caused Mary to conceive, or that God deposited the body of His Son in the womb of Mary. But as we said earlier, Mary conceived and Jesus was called the Son of God because Holy Spirit overshadowed Mary, not because of the origin of the seed.

Remember also, if God brought the seed from heaven or anywhere *outside of the earth* or *from anyone who was not Adam, Eve, or in their lineage*, He violated the blessing He spoke over the man and the woman. He would have entered the earth *apart and separate from their mandate to be fruitful and multiply*. God was not working apart from or superseding the procreative order He established in Genesis; *He was working through it*. If He did not, the birth of Christ would have been an illegal entry into the creation just like to progeny of the sons of God in Genesis 6.

So, how could God cause Mary to miraculously conceive in the earth without violating His original blessing and the "*be fruitful and multiply*" mandate that He gave mankind? As we said a moment ago, He moved on earth and *outside of time* to take the seed from the sinless pre-fall Adam He blessed to be fruitful and multiply, overshadowed Mary with it *in the fullness of time*, and caused her to conceive. That truly made Jesus the Son of God because of *where He came from*, the Son of Man because of *where the seed came from*, and our kinsmen redeemer with no *iniquitous history* or *sin nature* to pass on.

By taking the seed from a sinless, pre-fall Adam: 1. Jesus would still be the *Word made flesh*, 2. Mary would still experience a miraculous *virgin conception and birth*, 3. Jesus would truly and physically be the genetic *Son of Man*, 4. Jesus would truly be the *Last Adam* born genetically of the first Adam, 5. There was no *sin nature or iniquitous genetic history* in the seed to pass on during conception, and 6. Jesus would still be called the *Son of God* because of Holy Spirit's involvement in the conception and His personal, pre-incarnate existence as God.

When Mary miraculously conceived by Holy Spirit, a *Son of Man* body was genetically formed in her womb as the genesis of restored humanity, a true genetic descendant of pre-fall, first Adam. The *Son of God* then left heaven and His unified relationship with His Father and Holy Spirit to descend into genetically conceived flesh as the Word made flesh, the Son of Man, the Last Adam (John 1:14; Philippians 2:5-7).

Jesus had to be the Son of Man to legally enter the creation given to man. The Bible refers to the first Adam as *the man* and Jesus as the *Son of Man*. In fact, the entire Genesis narrative first refers to Adam as *man*: Let us make *man*, God formed *man*, *man* became a living being, the Lord God took the *man*, and the Lord God commanded the *man*, and, it is not good that *man* should be alone (Genesis 1 and 2). Then, when the angel visited Mary and told her she would conceive, she responded by saying she had not known a *man*. The angel told her she would conceive by the power of the Holy Spirit (Luke 1). When Holy Spirit overshadowed Mary, she miraculously conceived by way of the seed of the first *man*. When Jesus was born of the seed of that *man*, He became the Son of *Man*. You cannot be the Son of *Man* unless your father *is a man*. The *Son of God* (spiritually — from heaven) and the *Son of Man* (genetically — from the original man) merged to become one: fully God and fully *man*. I submit that:

> Jesus is called the Son of *Man* because of where the *SEED* came from.
> Jesus is called the Son of *God* because of where *HE* came from.

The Son of God became the Son of Man. Christ, as the Last Adam, became the fulfillment of all the first Adam failed to do so God could bring His lost son and family back into relationship with Himself, and with heaven, through an Adam-for-Adam reversal. Jesus left His estate in heaven, entered the earth and took up residence in, and as Adam, to walk out the fulfillment of God's original plan and destiny for mankind. As the Word made flesh, Jesus was the genetic progeny, expression, and reintroduction of Adam with the same choice to make as the first Adam. *But this time, the Son of God from heaven who merged with an Adamic genetic structure to be the Son of Man, overcame.*

I recognize this thought does not tow the institutional line and may be considered heretical by some, but please understand that I am not questioning or denying the divinity of Christ, or that He is both the *Son of God* and the *Word made flesh*. I am not denying His pre-incarnate existence as God. I am not denying His miraculous conception and miracle birth. I am simply offering another possibility as to where the sinless genetic seed came from to form the earthen vessel the *Son of God* descended into to become the *Son of Man* — *from the sinless and genetically pure first Adam before the fall, that is why He is the Last Adam.*

3 : HOW CHRIST CAME

When God created woman, He brought her from Adam's side. He did not form her from the dust of the creation like He did Adam. Why not? Because He had already deposited the genome that all humanity would come from in the body/blood of the first Adam. He merely removed a portion to create woman from the same genetic material. The woman was then the genetically comparable female equivalent of Adam (Genesis 2:18). Their assignment was to be fruitful and multiply to populate the earth with additional expressions of the image of God He invested in them.

I believe when God caused a deep sleep to fall on Adam to create the woman, He also secured and preserved a pure genetic seed that He knew would eventually be corrupted by the fall. He secured a seed that could and would be corrupted before it was corrupted. God would later bring that uncorrupted genetic seed into the fullness of time to cause Mary — who carried the seed of the woman — to conceive and give birth to the Son of God, as the Son of Man, for our full redemption. Let's modify something we said in Chapter Two:

> God did not start over with the Last Adam.
> He redeemed humanity and the creation through Him.
> Jesus is called the Last Adam because He was God's Son, Adam's genetic son, and the reintroduction of God's original plan for humanity.

God did not start over; He redeemed mankind and the creation through the Last Adam. When God secured that seed, He preserved it to become the genesis of our genetic redemption and the seed by which Christ would be born of a virgin. He was the true genetic first-born son of pre-fall, first Adam. In the same way, He used the original DNA from the man to create the woman, He used the original DNA from the man He made in His image to construct the earthen vessel the Son of God descended into to become the Son of Man. All to redeem humanity and the creation. God did not introduce a new genetic stream into the earth, *He reintroduced the perfection of the original genome before it was corrupted and reprogrammed by the law of sin and death.*

CHAPTER 4: WHY CHRIST CAME

The reality of *why* Christ came as the Word made flesh is strongly linked to *how* He came to be the Word made flesh. At the end of Chapter 3, we summed up *how* He became flesh by saying, "In the same way He used the original DNA from the man to create the woman, He used the original DNA from the man He made in His image to construct the earthen vessel the Son of God descended into to become the Son of Man. All to redeem humanity and the creation. God did not introduce a new genetic stream into the earth, *He reintroduced the perfection of the original genome before it was corrupted and reprogrammed by the law of sin and death.*"

Christ's birth as the genetic descendant of the first Adam put Him in the unique position to walk out the same journey as the first Adam. Why is being born of the first Adam, *the first man*, important? Let's answer that by starting with this verse.

> He is the image of the invisible God, the firstborn over all creation.
> Colossians 1:15

Paul said Jesus is the image of the invisible God, the firstborn over all creation. In Chapter 2, we said: "DNA is the fabric of creation and the method God used to encode His unseen immeasurable nature in the visible world." Our whole discussion of DNA has been that God expressed Himself in the living creation through DNA. So then Jesus, being born of original DNA from pre-fall Adam, became the image of the invisible God the way the first Adam expressed the image of the invisible God when God formed him from the dust of the creation (Genesis 1:26; 2:7).

Just like Paul mentioned the image of God in Colossians 1:15, so does Hebrews 1:1-3: The writer of Hebrews said:

> God, who at various times and in various ways spoke in time past to the fathers by the prophets, has in these last days spoken to us by His Son, *whom he has appointed heir of all things*, through whom also He made the worlds; who being the brightness of His glory and *the express image of His person.* (emphasis added)

Paul and the writer of Hebrews declared Jesus to be the image of the invisible God, and the express image of God's person. But in Colossians 1:15, Paul not only referred to Jesus as the image of the invisible God, he also referred to Jesus as the *firstborn over all creation*.

That statement is very important to our understanding of why Christ came as not only the Son of God, but also the genetic son of the first Adam. The first Adam was never called the firstborn over all creation even though he was given dominion over all creation. Why not? Because the first Adam was not born; *he was created.*

When Jesus was born of the seed of pre-fall Adam, He literally became the firstborn son of pre-fall, sinless Adam. He became the firstborn son of the man God placed in the garden before the fall. That made Jesus the *firstborn over creation and Adam's righteous and rightful heir.* The seed of pre-fall Adam preceded the birth of all post-fall humanity. *Adam and Eve's children were all born of post-fall seed.* As a result, the moment Jesus was born of pre-fall seed, the moment the Word of God became flesh of pre-fall seed, He inherited the creation as the living firstborn descendent of His biological, genetic, pre-fall, earthly father. The scriptural pattern throughout the Bible is exceedingly clear, the firstborn son inherits what belongs to the father. God gave the first Adam dominion over the creation, and as Adam's firstborn genetic son, the Man, Jesus of Nazareth, inherited that creation from Adam. As further confirmation of this truth, the writer of Hebrews not only said Jesus was the express image of God's person, he also said Jesus was *appointed heir of all things. Jesus inherited all things!*

4 : WHY CHRIST CAME

God was wise enough to preempt the planned deception of the enemy. When He secured that seed, He ensured that Adam would have a righteous firstborn heir regardless of the fall. The amount of chronological time that passed between the death of the first Adam and the birth of the Last Adam is irrelevant. The seed that caused Mary to conceive was not time-based. It entered time, when the fullness of time had come, from a place before the fall so it made Christ Adam's rightful, pre-fall heir, the moment He was born.

Christ's right to inherit the creation preceded the fall. Since Christ was a pre-fall heir by way of pre-fall seed, He also has the right and responsibility to return the creation to its pre-fall condition.

> Christ's death, burial, and resurrection did not make Him the heir or firstborn over all creation; His birth as the genetic son of Adam did. His death, burial, and resurrection made us joint-heirs.

Christ inherited the creation at His birth. When He did, it came into the possession of God's only-begotten Son like it had been in the possession of God's only-created son before the fall. That means the pre-fall heir inherited a post-fall creation with a plan to redeem it and a right to restore it. Christ inherited the fallen creation at His birth. As the Son of Man, *Christ inherited the creation at His birth and redeemed the creation He inherited at the cross*. The creation is now waiting earnestly for the revealing of the sons of God to enforce the blood-bought redemption and restoration of Christ's inheritance. The creation belongs to Christ and it belongs to us. It is our inheritance as joint heirs with Christ.

> The Spirit Himself bears witness with our spirit that we are children of God, and if children, *then heirs — heirs of God and joint-heirs with Christ.*
> Romans 8:16–17 (emphasis added)

We are joint heirs with Christ to inherit what Christ inherits. This is what God told the Messiah to ask for:

> Ask of Me, and I will give you the nations for *your inheritance*,
> and the ends of the earth for your possession.
> Psalm 2:8 (emphasis added)

God, speaking of the Messiah, said to ask Him for the nations as an inheritance and the ends of the earth for a possession. *The nations are people groups with a genome, and the earth is the creation and our possession.* God told the Messiah to ask Him for what was rightfully His. But now, just like when Israel crossed the Jordan, giants are in possession of our mutual inheritance. The giants are the current world systems built on the fallen human genome and man's thoughts and ways. Our role as inheritors and sons is to *merge heaven and earth* through our unified relationship *with God and with each other.*

The first reason Jesus was born of the seed of pre-fall Adam was to make Him the *firstborn* and *legitimate heir* over all creation. The second reason is so Jesus, the Last Adam, would face the same scenario the first Adam faced for the full redemption of mankind and the creation.

As we said earlier, the DNA and genome for the entire human race was resident within the genome of Adam when God created him. That means when Jesus was the firstborn of pre-fall Adam, the DNA and genome of the entire human race was also present in Him when He was born. Why is that important you ask? Because it means we literally existed in Christ genetically like we existed in the first Adam genetically. *We were genetically with Christ when He was conceived, when He was born, when He was baptized, when He was crucified, and when He was resurrected.*

All humanity that would ever live would come from the genome in the first Adam. As a result, all humanity that would ever live was resident within the genome of Christ as his firstborn son, even those who had already been born of the fallen first Adam. That is why all humanity fell with the first Adam and all humanity can be restored through the Last Adam. Because the seed that caused Mary to conceive entered time from a place before the fall *and before the post-fall multiplication of humanity*, the genome in Christ preceded the subsequent birth, life, and death of every generation born of the fallen seed and altered genetics of Adam.

4 : WHY CHRIST CAME

Everyone who accepts Christ was crucified with Him. Because He was the firstborn of pre-fall Adam, His genetic structure contained the whole of unborn humanity before the law of sin and death entered the equation. We were literally in Him on the cross the way we were genetically in Adam at the fall. As we said in Chapter 2, this same truth is evident with Abraham and Levi also. "Even Levi, who receives tithes, paid tithes through Abraham, so to speak, for he was still in the loins of his father when Melchizedek met him" (Hebrews 7:9-10).

The writer of Hebrews said Levi paid tithes to Melchizedek because he was in the loins, the genome, of his father Abraham when Abraham gave a tithe to Melchizedek. Likewise, the whole human race was in the loins, the genome of Christ, when He was crucified as the first-generation, righteous descendant of pre-fall Adam.

That is how we were crucified with Christ. We were literally in Him genetically when He was crucified. But we must go further yet to gain a greater understanding of the typology of the first and Last Adams and the Son-for-son reversal that secured our redemption. We must move beyond our initial comparisons of the first and Last Adams into a deeper revelation that reveals Jesus as the complete fulfillment of the type that was the first Adam.

Proverbs 25:2 declares, "It is the glory of God to conceal a matter and the glory of kings to search it out." That verse means we must go deeper to see what God has *concealed* in His Word. This does not refer to a surface revelation, but to deeper truths. To find the deeper truths, we must begin with the understanding that unless Jesus followed the same pattern and faced the same scenario as the first Adam, He could not truly be the Last Adam.

For Jesus, the Last Adam, to do what the first Adam failed to do, He had to face what the first Adam faced. If their journeys were not the same, then one could not be a true one-for-one type of the other and they could not both be Adams. They would be two different people on two different journeys with no "typology" involved in the dynamics of their individual purposes. But the reality is, they both had the same destiny and purpose: *to be fruitful and multiply, to fill the earth with the image and likeness of God, and to subdue it.*

The exception is that God did not create Jesus from the dust of the creation like He created Adam. The genetic structure for humanity was already in the earth and that is what God used. God combined the pre-fall seed and genetics from the first Adam with the genetics that contained the inactive record of sin and death encoded in the seed of the woman, Mary. Jesus left heaven "*as God*" to descend into a miraculously conceived genetic expression of both pre-fall and post-fall humanity. As the Son of God, Jesus left heaven to be Adam's Son of Man descendent and our kinsmen redeemer (Genesis 2:7; Luke 1:26-35; 1 Corinthians 15:47; Philippians 2:6).

While living in a body with both pre-fall and post-fall genetics, Jesus had the specific assignment of remaining humbled and hidden *in the appearance of man* while simultaneously reversing the actions of the first Adam to reconcile man back to God (Philippians 2:8). Christ's assignment required Him to pass through this life as the Last Adam and to face and overcome where the first Adam failed; *all to put us back on track with our eternal purpose as sons of God*. Now the questions are, "What did He face that the first Adam faced and what did He overcome and how?"

Let's start with this: To redeem a fallen body, Jesus had to inhabit a body with fallen potential and fallen genetics. If He did not, a fallen body would not be a part of His death, burial, and resurrection. A body that contained fallen genetics, *although without an activated sin nature*, needed to be a part of the process or it could not be nailed to the cross and subsequently resurrected. Jesus could not redeem what He did not embody.

Since it is the male seed that activates the sin nature, the sin nature resident in Mary's fallen DNA was not activated in the body of Jesus. Jesus was born of a pre-fall uncorrupted genetic male seed that did not contain a sin nature. Therefore, He would have had to willingly choose to sin (like the first Adam) to activate that nature within Mary's genetic contribution to His earthen vessel. Since eating of the tree brought genetic degradation through the first Adam, activating the dormant sin nature embedded in Mary's genetic contribution to His body — through sin — would have been the same as eating of the tree of the knowledge of good and evil for the Last Adam. Jesus faced the same genetic scenario internally the first Adam faced externally. If Jesus had sinned, He would have activated the inactive law of sin and death resident in Mary's genetic contribution to His body.

4 : WHY CHRIST CAME

> So when the woman saw that the tree was good for food, that
> it was pleasant to the eyes, and a tree desirable to make one wise,
> she took of its fruit and ate.
> *She also gave to her husband with her, and he ate.*
> Genesis 3:6 (emphasis added)

Here is the scenario: The woman who was created from Adam's genome was deceived and ate before Adam ate. She stood before Adam with the source of sin already *in her body and genome* while Adam remained pure before God. Adam's eyes were not opened because of the woman's actions; he had to exercise his own will and choose to partner with her to separate himself from God and take on the same fallen genetic condition. When Jesus descended into an earthen vessel, that vessel contained the same genetic scenario internally. The *pre-fall seed* that caused Mary to conceive was pure before God just like pre-fall Adam, but occupied the same body as the inactive fallen genetics contributed by Mary. Mary's inactive fallen genetics in Christ's body represented fallen Eve standing with Adam before he ate of the tree.

That is the scenario. The Son of God from heaven descended into and occupied a body that contained both the pre-fall sinless genetic seed of the first Adam and the inactive fallen genetics of mankind brought to Him by Mary. He descended into a body that contained a genetic record of both the original image of God *and* the inactive law of sin and death. What did He do? He drew on His relationship and revelation of God to reject the record of sin and death brought to Him genetically by Mary. The first Adam could have drawn on his revelation and relationship with God to reject the source of sin brought to him in the garden, the same way Jesus rejected the inactive fallen nature brought to Him genetically by Mary.

Stated simply, Jesus chose to partner with His Heavenly Father, be led by the Spirit, and reject any form of disobedience. The Last Adam chose to reject the inactive record of sin and death embedded in the genetic contribution of mankind brought to His body through Mary. All so He could fully redeem the first Adam and his faith-filled believing descendants. The Last Adam redeemed the first Adam and in so doing, redeemed all believing humanity. It was a reset that superseded time to include those of faith who had already died.

If Jesus did not descend into and inhabit a body that included fallen genetics, *although inactive*, He could not carry those fallen genetics to the cross. Jesus escorted the inactive iniquitous record of sin and death He overcame to the cross where He abolished them in His flesh. Jesus voluntarily suffered the agony of the crucifixion to nail the law of sin and death encoded in our fallen genome back to the tree they came from. He rose with only one genetic record: a pure genetic record that had no record of sin, death, or iniquitous history. He left fallen humanity's genetic contribution to His earthen vessel on the cross. *His resurrected body bore the image and likeness of God without a genetic record of sin or death.*

Paul said Jesus abolished *"in His flesh"* (His incarnate body) the enmity, that is, *the law of commandments contained in ordinances,* so as to create in Himself *one new man* from the two (Jew and Gentile), thus making peace, that He might reconcile them both to God *in one body* through the cross, thereby putting to death the enmity (Ephesians 2:15).

What Jesus did was incredible. He reunited humanity and made *one new man* in *one body*, out of Jew and Gentile. Just like there was initially only one body with the first Adam, there is only one body with the Last Adam. Paul said Jesus, the Last Adam, abolished *in His flesh* the law of commandments. How did He abolish the law of commandments *in His flesh*, in one body? He nailed the fallen genetic code, the record of sin, death, and separation from God of all men, Jew and Gentile, to the cross and left it there. All believing humanity, Jew, and Gentile, are now one body. We are one body and one blood, the body and blood of Christ, the Last Adam.

> *He who knew no sin became sin*
> *so we might become the righteousness of God in Him.*
> *2 Corinthians 5:21 (emphasis added)*

Paul also said that Jesus, *who knew no sin*, became sin. How did He become sin? Before He gave up the ghost and left His body, He allowed the sin nature and record of death in His body, *in His flesh*, to become active on the cross so it could be nailed to the cross. Jesus allowed His body, His flesh, *to become the body of sin* so He could condemn sin in His flesh (Romans 8:3). When He did, He felt the reality of sin and death and the sudden absence of the image and likeness of God in His very being the same way Adam did when his eyes were opened at the fall. He felt separation from God and what life was like with a fallen genome overtaken by sin and death without the glory of His Father. He felt what life was like without the living presence of God contained in the very depth of His being, the depth of His body, the depth of His genome. "My God, My God, why have You forsaken Me?" (Matthew 27:46)

When Jesus became sin, and died, He fulfilled the law *of sin and death* when He put the *body of sin* He became *to death*. It is no coincidence that Adam ate of a tree and Jesus died on a tree. The truth is, all unborn humanity was in, and with, both Adams genetically when they did what they did. We were genetically in Adam when he ate of the tree, and genetically in Jesus when He abolished and nailed our record of sin back to the tree. Paul said,

> Or do you not know that as many of us as were baptized into Christ Jesus *were baptized into His death? Therefore, we were buried with Him through baptism into death, that just as Christ was raised from the dead by the glory of the Father, even so, we also should walk in newness of life.* For if we have been united together in the likeness of His death, certainly we also shall be in the likeness of His resurrection, know this, that *our old man (our genetic record — author added) was crucified with Him, that the body of sin (the genetic record — author added) might be done away with* that we should no longer be slaves of sin.
> Romans 6:3-6 (emphasis added)

We have been crucified, buried, and resurrected to new life in Christ and the body of sin has been done away with. Jesus literally became sin. *He became the full expression of the genetic body of sin.* After they nailed Jesus to the cross, He *allowed* the sin nature to become active and the genetic body of sin to fully manifest the law of sin and death in His flesh. But because the body of Christ was nailed to the cross, the genetic body of sin He became could not slither off the altar it was nailed to. *He became the genetic body of sin to condemn sin in the flesh, and to nail sin and the fallen genome He became back to the tree they came from. He nailed the fallen genetic code bearing the record of sin and death to the cross and left it there.*

Now we have been offered restored genetics as a redemptive option. An option? Yes, an option. We can still choose to identify with the body of sin and the law of sin and death through the genetic contribution of our parents. We can still choose to identify with the memories of the body of sin, and the law of sin and death, over the incorruptible seed that is the Word of God. We can choose the genetics of our natural parents over the law of the Spirit of life in Christ, which made us free from the law of sin and death. We can choose to wait for the long-awaited catching away of the church rather than access what Christ has made available now through faith and our new genetic lineage. I believe that is one aspect of what Jesus meant when He said,

> To him who overcomes I will grant to sit with Me on My throne, as I also overcame and sat down with My Father on His throne.
> Revelation 3:21

What does it mean to overcome? To overcome is to reject the iniquitous genetic history and record passed down from our parents in favor of God's incorruptible seed that is the Word of God. We can reject the genetic history of our parents just like Jesus overcame by rejecting the inactive fallen genetics from Mary. Genetics were designed to house the image and likeness of God in partnership with our consciousness. Together they were to be the gateway of manifestation for the Word of God through the physical body of mankind. Our whole being was designed to express God's image and likeness, not just the spirit or soul of man.

To overcome means that we reject the old and all that is from our former fallen nature and self-image. To overcome means we embrace what God has done for us, who He is in us, and His Word, so we can fully express His image, likeness, thoughts, and ways to the creation.

Our sin nature and fallen genetic record was crucified with Christ and the body of sin was done away with. Because the body of sin was crucified and done away with, we can, by faith, identify with our kinsmen redeemer, the Adam who never fell. We are now born of incorruptible seed that is the Word of God. We have been realigned and regenerated. God has merged our identity and the nature of our very existence with Himself in Christ. God has merged with us through Christ to express Christ through us.

4 : WHY CHRIST CAME

Cain and Abel were not first generation descendants of Adam as we suppose. Cain and Abel were *first de-generation descendants* of the fallen first Adam, with a fallen human nature and genome. Jesus was a sinless *first generation descendent* of sinless pre-fall Adam. When we are born of incorruptible seed that is the Word of God, we become sinless *first re-generation descendants* of the Adam who never fell because He not only redeemed our fallen human nature, *but our fallen genome as well.*

True manifest sonship is to be a fully matured, *spiritually realigned genetic descendant* of the Adam who never fell. The order of Melchizedek: "without father, without mother, without genealogy, having neither beginning of days nor end of life but made like the son of God" (Hebrews 7:3)

CHAPTER 5: THE ORDER OF SACRIFICE

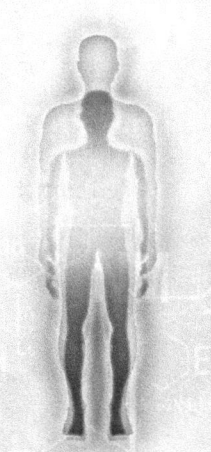

When we see a first in scripture, something mentioned or observed for the first time, it is important for us to pay attention to it. It is especially important when interpreting scripture, developing doctrine, and/or correlating events and observed patterns in the Bible. It is called the law of first mention. That is what we are doing here as we look at the first two recorded deaths in scripture. *The first death was a lamb; the second death was a man.*

> Now Adam knew Eve his wife, and she conceived and bore Cain, and said, "I have acquired a man from the Lord." Then she bore again, this time his brother Abel. *Now Abel was a keeper of sheep*, but Cain was a tiller of the ground. And in the process of time, it came to pass that Cain brought an offering of the fruit of the ground to the Lord. *Abel also brought of the firstborn of his flock and of their fat.* And the Lord respected Abel and his offering, *but He did not respect Cain and his offering. And Cain was very angry, and his countenance fell.*
> Genesis 4:1-5 (emphasis added)

Here we see the first recorded death in the Bible is the death of an animal. Abel brought the Lord an offering, a lamb. God accepted Abel's offering but rejected the offering of his older brother, Cain. At the end of verse 5, Cain was very angry because God did not respect his offering. In verse 8, that anger manifested as a murderous act.

> Now Cain talked with Abel his brother; and it came to pass, when they
> were in the field, that *Cain rose up against Abel his brother and killed him.*
> Genesis 4:8 (emphasis added)

Here we see the first recorded death of a human being. Cain killed his brother Abel; a shepherd. How interesting. The first two deaths recorded in scripture are a lamb and a shepherd. It does not take much effort to conclude that Jesus was later personified as the Lamb that was slain and the Good Shepherd who gave His life for the sheep. When Jesus was crucified, He was both the Lamb of God and the Good Shepherd. He merged and personified the first two deaths in the Bible to restore the order of sacrifice with the heavenly pattern. Now let's look at this in greater detail.

Beginning with Revelation 5:1, the Book of Revelation makes 29 references to the Lamb of God. In Revelation 5:6, John said the Lamb had the appearance of having been slain. In Revelation 13:8, John said the Lamb had been slain from, or, before the foundations of the world. Furthermore, John the Baptist identified Jesus as the Lamb of God (John 1:29).

> And I looked, and behold, in the midst of the throne and of the four living
> creatures, and in the midst of the elders, *stood* **a Lamb** *as though it had
> been slain,* having seven horns and seven eyes,
> which are the seven Spirits of God sent out into all the earth.
> Revelation 5:6 (emphasis added)

> All who dwell on the earth will worship him,
> whose names have not been written in the Book of Life
> of **the Lamb** slain from the foundation of the world.
> Revelation 13:8 (emphasis added)

> The next day John saw **Jesus** coming toward him, and said,
> "Behold! **The Lamb** of God who takes away the sin of the world!"
> John 1:29 (emphasis added)

The Book of Revelation reveals the Lamb of God was slain for the foundations of the world and John the Baptist identified Jesus as that Lamb. Without an understanding of the order of sacrifice in the heavens and the earth, depictions of Jesus as man and lamb can be a difficult concept to grasp. I think the clarity lies in the interaction between Cain, Abel, and God.

Let's begin with the context of Genesis 4, a *discussion between God and Cain regarding his offering.* Cain was a tiller of the ground and brought an offering of the fruit of the ground. Abel was a tender of sheep and brought an offering of the firstborn of his flock. God accepted Abel's sacrifice. Why did God accept Abel's sacrifice? I believe it was accepted because it followed the heavenly pattern. The Lamb of God was slain before the foundations of the world and Abel brought a lamb, a blood-based, fruit of the womb offering that followed that pattern. God did not accept Cain's offering and told him that if he did well, he would be accepted, if he did not do well, sin was lying at the door. Cain did not do well and sin entered.

The next thing we see is that Cain killed Abel. What is important here is that we see the context of this entire passage *is an offering; a sacrifice before the Lord.* Before Cain returned to offer any other sacrifice that might be acceptable to God, Cain killed his brother Abel. Abel was a tender of sheep; *Abel was a shepherd.* How interesting, Abel the shepherd *slew a lamb,* but Cain a tiller of the ground *slew a shepherd. The offering of a shepherd was a blood-based, fruit of the womb offering. Cain's offering of Abel was a higher order of sacrifice in the creation than Abel's offering of a lamb.*

As we said earlier, according to Dr. Ogbonnaya, the shedding of the blood of the Lamb of God brought the creation from the unseen to the seen realm.[3] Once the creation was in the seen realm, *God gave man dominion over it.* As a result, creation was subject to the authority, rule, and dominion of humanity. Cain had authority in the creation and his actions affected the order of things within the creation. When Cain killed Abel, he introduced *to the already created realm,* human sacrifice as a blood-based, fruit of the womb offering. *Human sacrifice, in one form or another, then became the sacrificial standard in the fallen creation.*

The killing of Abel became the foundation for how fallen humanity would operate in the earth from that point forward. Kingdoms would be built on people and their blood rather than the foundation God laid for the creation with the blood of the Lamb. Since

---

3   www.Aactev8.com

that time, willful acts of violence and the shedding of blood have been the sacrifice-based instrument of change used to orchestrate the agendas of the kingdom of darkness and fallen humanity. In fact, Cain built a city after he killed Abel. Abel's blood was foundational to that city. Furthermore, that is what wars are all about. People are sacrificed in exchange for what governments and the elite ruling class desire to gain or retain. By killing Abel, Cain increased the level of the blood-based, fruit of the womb offering from that of a lamb, according to the heavenly pattern, to that of a man as the new earthly order.

That sacrifice established a foundation and order of life that all present-day world systems operate on: preying on the blood and fallen genome of humanity. Whether it was an intentional sacrifice or not, the shedding of blood is deemed a sacrifice *and the ground opened its mouth to receive the blood of Abel.* Abel was a shepherd who offered a sacrifice God received; Cain was a tiller of the ground who offered a sacrifice the ground received. God received Abel's blood sacrifice. But the ground, *the creation*, received Cain's blood sacrifice.

> So now you are cursed from the earth, which has opened its mouth
> to receive your brother's blood from your hand.
> Genesis 4:11

The earth opened its mouth to receive the blood of Abel, *a shepherd*. The next question is, "How deep into the earth did Abel's blood flow?" I cannot say, but it clearly affected the order of life in the earth in ways not introduced or supported by the blood of the Lamb. God Himself said the earth opened its mouth to receive Abel's blood and when it did, that blood took up residence in the earth.

When we open our mouths and receive something, it has systemic implications for our bodies. If we take a drink of water, it affects our whole body based on what is in the water. In the same way our bodies receive water, I believe the earth received the blood of Abel with fallen genetics. Those fallen genetics had a systemic effect on the created realm and established an order of life based on the contents of the blood of fallen humanity. As we said in Chapter 2:

5 : THE ORDER OF SACRIFICE

> Whether we recognize it or not, the world and the current world systems have been built on fallen DNA. Every system exploits the fallen genetics of man as a revenue stream and means of control.
> The world is sacrificing and trading on your blood and the fallen genetics within it to create wealth.

The death of Abel has three observable repercussions: 1. Cain increased the level of blood-based sacrifice *in the earth/creation* from the heavenly order of a lamb, to the earthly order of a shepherd, 2. It violated the order of "man as shepherd" and "lamb as sacrifice" to set a new order of "*man as lamb and sacrifice*" and 3. The created realm opened its mouth to receive the spilled blood of Abel as its operational foundation rather than the blood of the Lamb of God that manifested the creation.

The blood of Jesus was *on* the foundation stone of creation, but the foundation *in* the created realm was now realigned based on a blood sacrifice *offered within the created realm: the blood of a shepherd with fallen genetics*. Cain opened a gateway; a door, that granted entrance to a new level of sin and death in the created realm. The reality is that Cain did not merely open a door; he was the door that sin entered through. His sin granted entrance to greater sin. That anger-based sacrifice ushered in and gave entrance to a new world order that has found expression through various kingdoms, cultures, spiritual practices, secret societies, and governmental administrations throughout human history. All of them built on that pattern of sacrifice. That new sacrifice set the order for future world affairs and the necessity for a greater sacrifice in the created realm.

The only way God could reset the foundation *within the created realm* was to offer a better sacrifice than the blood of Abel *within the created realm*. God had to reintroduce the blood of the Lamb of God that was shed before the foundation of the created world, *into the created world*, to offer a better sacrifice than the blood of Abel offered by Cain. He did that through Jesus, the Lamb of God.

> ...to Jesus the Mediator of the new covenant,
> and to the *blood of sprinkling that speaks better things than that of Abel*.
> Hebrews 12:24 (emphasis added)

The writer of Hebrews makes it clear that the blood of Jesus speaks better things than the blood of Abel. Why did it speak better things? Because it contained the divine, sinless, genetic stream and image of God. That is one reason I believe Jesus was born of the seed of pre-fall Adam. That seed contained the genesis of the genetic redemption of humanity to speak better things than the blood of Abel with fallen genetics.

God had to increase the level of original sacrifice from a lamb *offered by* a shepherd with fallen genetics, to the sacrifice of the Lamb of God *as* a shepherd, the Good and Great Shepherd, with the original divine genetic stream shed before the foundation of the world. God had to bring a greater sacrifice than Cain made of Abel to realign the *created realm* with His original order. Jesus was the Lamb of God, the Good Shepherd, and the Great Shepherd who shed His blood. Blood that contained the life and light of the image and likeness of God.

The Gospel of John and the Book of Hebrews make it abundantly clear that Jesus was both the Lamb of God and the Good/Great Shepherd.

> The next day John saw Jesus coming toward him, and said, "Behold! *The Lamb* of God who takes away the sin of the world!"
> John 1:29 (emphasis added)

> I am the Good Shepherd. The *Good Shepherd* gives His life for the sheep.
> John 10:11 (emphasis added)

> As the Father knows Me, even so I know the Father; and *I lay down My life for the sheep.*
> John 10:15 (emphasis added)

> Now may the God of peace who brought up our Lord Jesus from the dead, that *Great Shepherd of the sheep, through the blood* of the everlasting covenant.
> Hebrews 13:20 (emphasis added)

In Exodus 4:22, God called the nation of Israel His son, *His firstborn*. That means the physical incarnation of Christ came after God declared Israel His firstborn. Chronologically speaking, Jesus was the younger brother of Israel. So, when the earthly priesthood put their younger brother Jesus to death, they slew the Good Shepherd just like Cain slew his younger brother Abel, who was a shepherd.

Jesus was the Lamb of God who remained humbled as the Son of Man. He was the Lamb of God slain before the foundation of the world, but this time, He was slain *in* the world so the earth could receive His blood the way it received the blood of Abel. But the blood of Jesus spoke of better things than the blood of Abel. Now, *we choose* which foundation we build and live on: the blood of Jesus and the Kingdom of God, or the blood of Abel and the kingdoms of this world.

When Jesus died, the earth received the blood of the Lamb of God slain before the foundations of the world; all so the Kingdom of God could be revealed in the created realm as God originally intended. Jesus said He is the resurrection and the life. When the earth received His blood, it brought resurrection life to those of faith who had already died. In partnership with the same Spirit that raised Christ from the dead, the blood of Jesus affected lives beneath the earth. "*And the graves were opened; and many bodies of the saints who had fallen asleep were raised; and coming out of the graves after His resurrection, they went into the holy city and appeared to many*" (Matthew 27:52-53). The blood of Jesus affected the lives of those who were beneath the earth.

While we have discussed two places where the blood of Jesus was applied, on the earth and beneath the earth, there is yet a third place the blood has been applied: in the holy place in heaven where He offered Himself as the sacrifice.

What Jesus did on the cross was a reset of the entire created realm: *under the earth* when the earth opened its mouth to receive the blood of Jesus the way it once received the blood of Abel, *in the earth* as the highest form of sacrifice when Christ was offered as the Great Shepherd and the Lamb of God on the cross, and *in the heavens* when He brought the blood of His own sacrifice *to the heavens*. This is evidenced by what Paul said in Philippians 2:8-11:

> And being found in appearance as a man, He humbled Himself and became obedient to the point of death, even the death of the cross. Therefore, God also has highly exalted Him and given Him the name, which is above every name, that at the name of Jesus every knee should bow, *of those in heaven*, and *of those on earth*, and *of those under the earth*, and that every tongue should confess that Jesus Christ is Lord, to the glory of God the Father.
> (emphasis added)

Paul makes it clear that because of Christ's death on the cross, He is exalted in three specifically identified realms: in heaven, on earth, and under the earth. That blood-based fruit of the womb offering and reset has given believing humanity access to all three realms as sons of our Father in heaven. As we said earlier, we were with Him on the foundation stone, we were with Him on the cross, and we are with Him in heaven. That gives us the authority to exercise dominion in all realms where Christ has dominion. We can now operate in, release, and build the Kingdom of God upon the reset foundation of the blood of the Lamb.

We cannot discuss the order of sacrifice and the blood of the Lamb without mentioning the power of communion to manifest that restored foundation, new genetic order, and regenerative potential in our lives.

> And He took bread, gave thanks and broke it, and gave it to them, saying, "This is My body which is given for you; do this in remembrance of Me." Likewise, He also took the cup after supper, saying, "This cup is the new covenant in My blood, which is shed for you."
> Luke 22:19–20

Jesus said, "This is My body which is given for you; do this in remembrance of Me." His body was His flesh. He also said, "This cup *is the new covenant in My blood*, which is shed for you." Jesus said that we are to receive His body and His blood. *Why would He give us His body and His blood if He were not redeeming our body and our blood?* Furthermore, when Jesus said we are to receive His body and His blood, He did not infer the elements were symbolic. That is not to say that they were literally flesh and blood, but more so, that God invested the divine genetic reality of His body and His blood into the bread and wine. When Jesus was crucified His body and His blood were separated. When we receive

5 : THE ORDER OF SACRIFICE

communion, they are reunited in us to release and enforce our restored unity with God, through Christ, to give us access beyond the veil.

Jesus made it clear that we are to receive His body and His blood. While many view communion as symbolic, Jesus placed a different emphasis on the elements than we do. He said: "*Most assuredly, I say to you, unless you eat the flesh of the Son of Man and drink His blood, you have no life in you. Whoever eats My flesh and drinks My blood has eternal life, and I will raise him up at the last day. For My flesh is food indeed, and My blood is drink indeed.*" From what Jesus said here in John 6:53-55, there is nothing symbolic about it.

While this may be new to us, receiving communion is the same as the earth opening its mouth to receive the blood of Jesus. The earth received His blood and so must we. When we receive communion, it is a faith-based gateway through which the living DNA of God, through Christ, enters our lives. We receive within ourselves the reality of the blood of Jesus as Christ's redemptive covenant with us.

Communion is a process that allows us to walk away from the memories of the body of sin stored genetically in our flesh, directly into the newness of life, the body of the resurrected Last Adam. We are not the body of Christ that walked the earth, *we are the resurrected body of Christ*. God gave us a way to remember the price Jesus paid for our redemption and to physically engage His redemptive incarnation. Consider all the places the blood is applied: on the foundation stone, beneath the earth, in the earth, and in heaven. Through communion, the blood is now applied in our lives to make us one with Christ and all the reconciled realms within Him. Remember what Paul said on Mars Hill? He said, "And He has made from *one blood* every nation of men to dwell on all the face of the earth." This time, God has made us a royal priesthood and a holy nation from one blood, His blood, *with the divine potential of His DNA* (1 Peter 2:9).

We are not finished though, there is more for us to see in this passage. In Luke 22:20, Jesus said, "*This cup is the new covenant in My blood.*" Notice that Jesus did not say the new covenant was sealed, ratified, or formalized with, or by, His blood. He said the new covenant is *in His blood*. What was and is in His blood? *The living DNA of God.* The DNA that was and is in His blood is encoded with the express image of God. I believe Jesus was telling us that the new covenant *in* His blood is the original DNA that God used to create mankind in His image.

A covenant is a contract, it is how an agreement is carried out and fulfilled. Historically, a blood covenant meant that if one party failed to fulfill the contract, it would cost them their life. With Jesus, however, He gave His life's blood and all it contained *as* the covenant and *as* the righteous, eternal, and *genetic contract* for our full redemption. When we receive communion, we are receiving the genetic contract God made to enable our bodies to fully express the form of God within us. *If the same Spirit that raised Christ from the dead dwells in you, He will quicken your mortal body* (Romans 8:22).

The same Spirit that raised Christ from the dead partners with us and enforces the genetic contract written in the blood of Jesus. The genetic contract in His blood is the law of the Spirit of life in Christ and the Word of God that speak better things than the law of sin and death encoded in the blood of Abel. *The law of the Spirit of life in Christ overwrites the memory of the law of sin and death recorded in our genome.* That is how we are transformed. We must understand that our blood has a genetic voice that is either quoting the law of sin and death or the blood of Jesus that speaks better things than the blood of Abel. When we believe, our genetic voice partners with the law of the Spirit of life in Christ and the Word of God to facilitate our transformation. It is a genetic alchemy.

How incredible. Jesus offered Himself as the Good Shepherd and the Lamb of God, all to reestablish the order of sacrifice and to reveal and release our true nature as sons of God through the genetic contract in His blood. His redemptive actions brought the creation full circle and made all that is necessary for our reset and realignment with God, and with heaven, available to us now.

I believe communion is a gateway to the fullness of the resurrected body of Christ, now. Why now? Because we are in the third day. Most of us are all familiar with 2 Peter 3:8.

> But beloved, do not forget this one thing, that with the Lord one day is as a thousand years and a thousand years as one day.

Many apply this scripture to the creation narrative, but we really cannot do that. We do not know how much time elapsed between Genesis 1:1-3. We do not know how much time elapsed between, "In the beginning, God created the heavens and the earth and the

5 : THE ORDER OF SACRIFICE

earth was without form and void" and day one of the creation narrative. We do know, however, that two millennial days have passed since the resurrection of Christ. We have entered the third millennial day; we are in the third day. Why is the third day important you ask? Because the body of Christ did not resurrect or participate in the finished work of Christ until the third day.

For the first two days, the body of Christ lay dormant in the grave while Jesus did what He did in the unseen realm. The body of Christ lay dormant for two days just like the body of the first Adam lay dormant after God formed him from the dust of the creation. As the Last Adam, the resurrection of Christ parallels the creation and entrance of life into the first Adam. The body of Christ was dead in the grave — and did not participate — just like the formed body of the first Adam was dead and did not participate until God breathed life into it. The life and resurrection of Christ was the fulfillment of the type that was the first Adam. When God breathed the breath of life into the first Adam, it was a prophetic demonstration of the future resurrection of Christ. Both Adam's had life come into a lifeless body. God breathing life into the first Adam was the creation of humanity, the resurrection of Christ was the birth of *new creation humanity*, more than the first Adam ever was (2 Corinthians 5:17).

On the third day, the unseen work Christ accomplished during the first two days was fully manifest as the resurrection. On the third day, Christ fully entered His body. On the third day, the resurrected Christ inhabited His body with His finished work and the fullness of His victory.

When Paul wrote to the church at Corinth, he said, "Now you are the body of Christ" (1 Corinthians 2:27). We are the body of Christ and this is the third day; it is the day Christ fully inhabits His body through resurrection. Christ fully inhabiting and resurrecting His body on *that* third day is how He is going to inhabit and resurrect the body of Christ on *this* third day. It is in this day the body of Christs get to fully express the resurrection power of the law of the Spirit of life in Christ in cooperation with the same Spirit that raised Christ from the dead. "But if the Spirit of Him who raised Jesus from the dead dwells in you, He who raised Christ from the dead will also give life to your mortal bodies through His Spirit who dwells in you" (Romans 8:11). The Spirit of God does not dwell in a dead body, He dwells in a mortal body to make it immortal. This is not talking about the resurrection of the dead in Christ after their deaths, this is talking about the transformation of our mortal bodies into the resurrected immortal body of Christ.

I strongly believe communion and receiving the body and blood of Christ is a gateway to that resurrection power — to the fullness of the third-day resurrected body of Christ. I encourage you to take communion often and in faith. I encourage you to engage and release the fullness of Christ's covenant within it, in partnership with the law of the Spirit of life in Christ. In so doing, you fully release the same Spirit that raised Christ from the dead into your physical body, to *transform* your body. It is a genetic reset that overwrites our genetic memory and partnership with the law of sin and death through the Word of God, to transform and transfigure us into the resurrected body of Christ, a holy nation, from one blood. *His blood.*

5 : THE ORDER OF SACRIFICE

CHAPTER 6: SIN AND DEATH

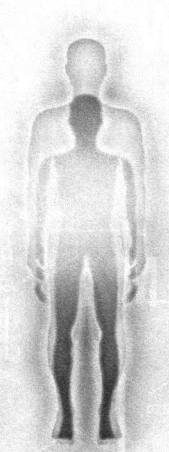

Rather than begin with the definition or origin of sin and death, I think we should start with God's answer to it: *the law of the Spirit of life in Christ.*

> For the law of the Spirit of life in Christ has made me free
> from the law of sin and death. Romans 8:2

Sin and death are a law. Our journey to understand the law of sin and death must begin with the understanding that the law of the Spirit of life in Christ conquered and supersedes that law. That is scripturally indisputable. Paul declared that Christ has made us free from the law of sin and death. You may ask, "How free?" Jesus answered that question Himself.

> Jesus answered them, "Most assuredly, I say to you, whoever commits sin
> is a slave of sin. And a slave does not abide in the house forever, but a son
> abides forever. Therefore, if the Son makes you free,
> you shall be free indeed.
> John 8:34-36

In that statement about freedom, Jesus was talking about one thing and one thing only - freedom from slavery to sin. Furthermore, Jesus emphasized that we are not merely free from sin, *but free indeed* as sons who abide in the house of His very being forever. *We are the body of Christ and we abide in Him.* So, it is an inarguable truth that the law of the Spirit of life in Christ has made us free *(and free indeed)* from sin, and by extension, the law of sin and death that abides in the body of unregenerate humanity because we have become the body of Christ.

As we continue, we need to briefly discuss three laws: *The Law of Moses, the law of sin and death,* and *the law of the Spirit of life in Christ.* First, *the Law of Moses* was not given to the Gentiles; therefore, its application is restricted to the Jews. Gentiles are not bound to keep the law, it is Jewish-centric in its application. Secondly, *the law of sin and death* applies to everyone, Jew, and Gentile. Thirdly, *the law of the Spirit of life in Christ* frees the Jew from the Law of Moses and frees everyone who accepts Christ (Jew and Gentile) from the law of sin and death. The law of the Spirit of life in Christ supersedes and makes us free from these laws, not free to sin, but free from the sin-based slavery genetically and consciously present within the body of sin.

In Romans 6, Paul emphasized our freedom from sin by declaring that the body of sin held captive by sin, has been done away with.

> For if we have been united together in the likeness of His death, certainly, we also shall be in the likeness of His resurrection, knowing this, *that our old man was crucified with Him, that the body of sin might be done away with, that we should no longer be slaves of sin.* For he who has died has been freed from sin.
> Romans 6:5-7 (emphasis added)

Paul and Jesus were talking about the same thing; freedom from sin and slavery to it. Paul said the body of sin (that was a slave to sin) has been done away with; it no longer exists. It is no longer our genetic identity or our master. Why? Because we were united with Christ in the likeness of His death and resurrection. As we said in Chapter 4, that is how Jesus has made us free from sin. We were all crucified with Him when He nailed the handwriting of ordinances that were against us, in His flesh, to the cross. While some may not agree that there is a genetic application or reality to sin, I believe the scriptures demonstrate there is.

In Romans 7, Paul talks about freedom from the law through death. He uses the

6 : SIN AND DEATH

example of marriage to show that death severs the relationship between the law and those bound by it.

> Or do you not know, brethren (for I speak to those who know the law), that the law has dominion over a man as long as he lives? For the woman who has a husband is bound by the law to her husband as long as he lives. But if the husband dies, she is released from the law of her husband. So then if, while her husband lives, she marries another man, she will be called an adulteress; but if her husband dies, she is free from that law, so that she is no adulteress, though she has married another man. *Therefore, my brethren, you also have become dead to the law through the body of Christ, that you may be married to another — to Him who was raised from the dead, that we should bear fruit to God.* For when we were in the flesh, the sinful passions which were aroused by the law were at work in our members to bear fruit to death. *But now we have been delivered from the law, having died to what we were held by so that we should serve in the newness of the spirit and not in the oldness of the letter.*
>
> Romans 7:1-6 (emphasis added)

While we could discuss this passage at length, we will limit the discussion to our main point. Those who have been crucified and resurrected with Christ are no longer bound by the Law of Moses, *or* the law of sin and death. Christ has made us free and *free indeed* from every law but the law of love. We are to love God and one another (Matthew 22:37-40). While Paul's discussion is specifically pointed at the Law of Moses, its application is much broader than the Law of Moses. How do we know that? Because of what Paul said in Romans 8:2, "For the law of the Spirit of life in Christ has made me free from the law of sin and death."

In essence, Jesus who knew no sin became the body and slave of sin with and for us, on the cross, to condemn that sin in His flesh to crucify and put it to death. When He did, He destroyed both the body of sin and the law of sin and death that were married at the fall. That body, that law, and that marriage no longer exist; they no longer apply to us. When Jesus became sin to do away with sin, He fulfilled the Law of Moses *through love,* and the law of sin and death *through and by His death.* Anyone connected or bound by either can now find freedom from them in Him and His resurrection. We have been freed from the body of sin to become the body of Christ which does not have a sin nature; *spiritually, soulishly, or genetically.*

In Romans 7, Paul was speaking from the position of a Jew who was endeavoring to keep the law, but could not. He then said the Jew was freed from the Law of Moses because their death in Christ severed their relationship with that law. But when Paul said the law of the Spirit of life in Christ has made me free from the law of sin and death, he broadened the application of the principle that death severs the connection to the Law of Moses for the Jew, in Romans 7, to everyone connected to the law of sin and death, in Romans 8. Whether Jew or Gentile, we are no longer married or connected to the Law of Moses or the law of sin and death. Jesus said He made us free from sin, Paul said Jesus made us free from the law of sin and death. We are free indeed! Now the question is, "What does that freedom look like?"

To answer that question, we must first answer these three questions, 1. Where the law of sin and death originated, 2. What the law of sin and death is, and 3. Where the law of sin and death resides. Paul clearly revealed where the law of sin and death entered the creation in Romans 5.

> Therefore, *just as through one man sin entered the world, and death through sin, and thus death spread to all men because all sinned.* For until the law sin was in the world, but sin is not imputed when there is no law. Nevertheless, death reigned from Adam to Moses, even over those who had not sinned according to the likeness of the transgression of Adam, who is a type of Him who was to come.
> Romans 5:12-14 (emphasis added)

1. The answer to our first question is: the law of sin and death originated with Adam. What is important to note here is that sin entered the world, and then death, through sin, spread to all men. *Death spreading to all men is the expression of the law of sin and death activated by the first Adam. It is a progressive death embedded in and enforced by the human genome and sin consciousness.*

It is also important to note that Paul said sin is not imputed where there is no law. The Law of Moses had not been given, that is why Paul said, "Nevertheless death reigned from

6 : SIN AND DEATH

Adam to Moses." The time from Adam to Moses is a time where there was no Law of Moses; therefore, sin was not imputed because sin is not imputed where there is no law. So, while sin was not imputed between the times of Adam and Moses where there was no law, the result of the first Adam's sin was nevertheless manifest from Adam to Moses because that death was genetic in nature. Whether there was an active law to impute sin was irrelevant at that point, *the genetic damage had been done.*

If sin is not imputed where there is no law, then what law did Adam transgress to *activate* the law of sin and death that spread to all men genetically? The answer is very simple.

> And the LORD God commanded the man, saying, "Of every tree of the garden you may freely eat; *but of the tree of the knowledge of good and evil you shall not eat, for in the day that you eat of it you shall surely die."* Genesis 2:16–17 (emphasis added)

2. The answer to our second question is: God's decree in Genesis 2 is the law of sin and death; if you eat you die. God gave a law, one law. He told the man he was not allowed to eat of the tree of the knowledge of good and evil. He then told him what would happen if he ate, he would die. The law was, don't eat. The sin or transgression was, eating. The sentence for transgressing the law of sin and death was, death.

The first Adam transgressed the law that said he was not allowed to eat of that tree. When he ate, he sinned; when he sinned, he activated the law of sin and death. The law he activated separated man from his unified relationship with God and opened the door to genetic death which then spread *genetically to all men.* As we said in Chapter 2, humanity was affected genetically by the fall of the first Adam. Adam's sin gave entrance to progressive degeneration leading to death.

Dr. Ogbonnaya teaches that the first Adam did not die because of what he consumed from the tree. He died because he activated the decree or law of God, "*for in the day you eat of it you shall surely die.*" Furthermore, Dr. Ogbonnaya defines death in the original language as "in dying, you will die and continue to die until you finally die."[4] That is the process of degeneration leading to death we mentioned in Chapter 2.

---

4   Aactev8.com

The sentence of progressive genetic death that Adam activated spread to all men through the procreative process as humanity multiplied to fill the earth. It spread to all men because the law of sin and death abides in the human genome. The human genome is the source of procreated life in the earth and the law of sin and death is epigenetically encoded in the human genome; it is therefore passed from generation to generation.

3. The answer to our third question is this: the law of sin and death resides in the human genome. The change in the human genome is what brought death and where sin and death manifested; death manifested in the physical body in partnership with the sin consciousness of humanity.

This is where I am going to drop a bomb on traditional thinking. I have used two terms throughout this book on purpose; the fallen nature of man and the fallen genome of man. Here is the bomb, they are one in the same. The fallen genome contains the fallen nature of man, the fallen nature of man is the fallen genome of man. The definition of fallen nature is then expanded beyond a genetic voice into a partnership with the fallen soul; together the body and soul of man comprise the fallen nature of man.

The human genome is the pool of genetic information that makes us who we are. If the law of sin and death is encoded in my genetic structures, then my blood speaks just like the blood of Abel in partnership with the soul and consciousness of my being. It speaks to me of sin and death. It does not have another script to draw from unless I choose to come into agreement with the law of the Spirit of life in Christ, in the body of Christ, as the body of Christ. As we said a moment ago, the law of sin and death is embedded in the human genome, the human body. Likewise, the law of the Spirit of life in Christ is in the body of Christ; we choose which body we operate from. I must choose to come into agreement with the redemptive work of Christ and His body so my blood has a new genetic voice to speak with.

When God decreed the law of sin and death, He was not speaking of a sudden death, but a death that would come progressively through degeneration ultimately leading to death. The reason people grow old and die is because the law of sin and death was activated by the first Adam.

We often view the first Adam's disobedience as the wholesale entrance of any and

6 : SIN AND DEATH

every kind of sin. We call it "original sin." But when God spoke with Cain in Genesis 4:7, He told Cain, "sin lies at the door." It is very clear that a measure, or type of sin, was present on the other side of a door awaiting entrance into the creation. The first Adam did not grant entrance to the sin that was waiting at that door, *Cain did*. That sin could not enter uninvited any more than degenerative death could enter without the first Adam's agreement. Adam's agreement activated the law of sin and death that spread to all men genetically. Cain's sacrifice of Abel amounted to a blood-based agreement with sin that opened the door to kingdom-building systemic sin. Original sin separated man from the living image of God *through Adam* to grant entrance to genetic degeneration leading to death. Likewise, Cain's sin and blood sacrifice of Abel granted entrance to sin *through Cain* as a systemic foundation that all world systems have been built on ever since.

The first Adam's sin granted entrance to death that spread to all men. Cain then used death to grant entrance to the kingdom of darkness. Adam's sin affected individual lives leading to degenerative death in partnership with human sin consciousness. Cain's sin granted entrance to a system and/or kingdom of sin that grew and spread to become present-day world systems — the kingdoms of this world.

God told Adam that if he ate of the tree he would die. As we said earlier, that means, "in dying you will die and continue to die until you finally die." God's sentence of death that spread to all men genetically through Adam was a progressive death, *not an instant death*. When Cain slew Abel, he violated God's decree of progressive death. *Cain introduced instant death that was not activated by Adam's transgression.* Instant death supersedes and violates God's decree of progressive death. The sentence of progressive degeneration leading to death provides an opportunity for progressive regeneration leading to life in Christ. Enoch is the perfect example of regeneration leading to life in Christ, even before the time of Christ. Progressive death affords an opportunity for repentance, restoration, growth, and maturity. Instant death closes the door on repentance and removes the potential for divine intervention and restoration.

Cain's use of instant death as a sacrifice granted wholesale entrance to the kingdom of darkness. That is why the blood sacrifice of Christ, the Lamb of God and Great Shepherd is two-fold: To reverse the law of sin and death introduced by the first Adam, *and*, to bring the Kingdom and will of His Father into the earth to replace the kingdoms built upon the blood sacrifice Cain made of Abel.

Here is the bottom line: God gave man dominion over the creation, but man sinned which then gave sin dominion over man through the law of sin and death in the human genome and consciousness. As a result, sin exercises dominion over the creation through enslaved humanity. Sin used enslaved humanity to build a systemic global kingdom with slavery to sin at its core. He who sins is a slave to sin. God, through Christ, then freed us from the law of sin and death and slavery to sin. Sin no longer has dominion over us so it can no longer have dominion over the creation through us to perpetuate its systemic hold on humanity. Since Christ made us free, and free indeed, God can and will release His Kingdom through us so it can be on earth as it is in heaven.

Abel's death and shed blood, at the hands of Cain, opened a door for systemic sin and the kingdom of darkness to enter the creation to build world systems. As we said earlier, it is interesting to note that Cain built a city after he killed his brother Abel, Abel's blood was foundational to that city. *Cain's city, Cain's community, and Cain's society was built on the sacrifice and shed blood of a human being.*

In the same way, Christ's death granted an ongoing, ever-increasing righteous entrance of the Kingdom of God into the creation through us by the shedding of His own blood. The shedding of His blood opened a gate. But this time, Jesus did not grant entrance to sin, He became sin: progressive degeneration leading to death from Adam, and the systemic kingdom-building sin from Cain. Because He *became sin*, He took sin out through the gate He opened by His own blood. *The Lamb of God who takes away the sin of the world.* The shadow of death and the genetic memory of the body of sin are all that remain — sin has been dealt with, conquered, and taken away by Christ. When Christ left this dimension at His death, *He took the sins of the world with Him — both individual sin and systemic kingdom building sin.*

It is time for us to recognize the scale of the redemption purchased by God through Christ and to step into the fullness of that redemption as sons of God who have been made free and free indeed. What is that freedom, that fullness? We will see as we discuss moving from the lesser works to operate in the greater works Jesus talked about in John 14:12.

CHAPTER 7: THE LESSER WORKS

I think it is best to begin with a definition of the lesser works. Stated plainly, the lesser works equate to *God anointing flesh.* He anoints flesh to allow us to deal with the issues resident within a world operating under the shadow of death until we become the light that fully reveals the image, likeness, and character of God. It is God anointing the sons of men. It is God pouring out His Spirit *on all flesh* according to Joel 2:2 and Acts 2:16-17.

> And it shall come to pass afterward that I will pour out My Spirit
> *on all flesh*; your sons and your daughters shall prophesy,
> your old men shall dream dreams, your young men shall see visions.
> Joel 2:28 (emphasis added)

> But this is what was spoken by the prophet Joel: And it shall come to pass
> in the last days, says God, *That I will pour out of My Spirit on all flesh*;
> your sons and your daughters shall prophesy, your young men
> shall see visions, your old men shall dream dreams.
> Acts 2:16-17 (emphasis added)

I am sure these next statements will raise the ire of some, but here goes: *being great at the lesser works is not the greater works, and more of the lesser works is not the greater works.* Old Testament saints operated with the anointing and New Testament saints operate with the anointing and gifts. *As new creatures in Christ Jesus, there is more available to us than the anointing and gifting.* The charismatic Church has focused primarily on developing spiritual gifts as the pinnacle of redemption and manifestation of the Kingdom of God until His return, *but it is not.*

I love Holy Spirit and the gifts He has graciously poured out on us. I am thankful God allows us to walk in them to demonstrate His love through healing and other restoring aspects of His nature. God gave us the gifts and *He wants us to continue to operate in the full grace and measure of His gifts*; but He never intended for the gifts to be our destination. They do not represent the fullness of *redemption*, *restoration*, or *regeneration*.

Sin and death have been dealt with, but world systems still operate within their shadow. The gifts of the Spirit are given to bring hope and healing to those still subject to the shadow of death until the resurrection power of Christ fully manifests in and through the body of Christ in the earth.

Furthermore, the Lord once told me the gifts of the Spirit are the *training wheels* of sonship. They are intended to allow us to experience the attributes and characteristics of sonship while maturing into it. He also said that what we do with those gifts demonstrates what we will do if He were to give us a kingdom. If we build *our own kingdom* with His gifts while operating in a world still dealing with the consequences of sin, under the shadow of death, then He cannot trust us *with the next and greater release of the His Kingdom*. Unfortunately, some have built their own ministry kingdoms with the gifts. Some have built kingdoms with the lesser works while abandoning the quest to understand and walk in the greater works. It seems there is no reason to move beyond the pinnacle of the lesser works when our needs are met and we find fulfillment, prosperity, and notoriety in the ministry we have built with them.

In part, I believe it is because we have not understood the greater works. I also believe it is a matter of God's timing for the release of the fullness of what He desires to manifest on earth today. After all, this is the third day. Nonetheless, we can still choose to remain great at the lesser works, or we can continue to operate in the lesser with our hearts set on the reality of moving into the greater works as Jesus said we would do.

The last few generations of Kingdom generals were amazing people who walked in

7 : THE LESSER WORKS

amazing levels of gifting with incredible hearts. I cannot emphasize enough that I respect them and give them the highest honor for their contributions to our corporate journey as the body of Christ.

We would not be where we are without them. You most likely know many of them by name: John Alexander Dowie (1847-1907), Maria Woodworth-Etter (1844-1924), John G. Lake (1870-1935), Smith Wigglesworth (1859-1947), William J. Seymour (1870-1922), Aimee Semple-McPherson (1890-1944), William Branham (1909-1965), Kathryn Kuhlman (1907-1976), A.A. Allen (1911-1970), Kenneth Hagin (1917-2003), Jack Coe (1918-1956), Oral Roberts (1918-2009), T.L. Osborne (1923-2013), R.W. Schambach (1926-2012), Bob Jones (1931-2014) and Dr. D.G.S. Dhinakaran (1935-2008).

What is interesting is this: if you were to mention these names to a group of believers, you would get a mixed reaction depending on individual belief systems and theological perspectives. Some would tell stories of their greatness and others of their failings. Did any of these people fail or walk in error along the way? Absolutely, but why did they falter? Because the gifts of the Spirit are not evidence that God is working *in or perfecting man*, they are evidence God is working *with man*. *God was with them just like He was with Jesus* (Acts 10:38). God poured out of His Spirit *on their flesh* and they developed the gifts He gave them to reveal a first-fruit expression of sonship and the Kingdom. Before you get upset and think I am diminishing the anointing, the gifts, or these generals, hear me out.

We must recognize that God pouring out of His Spirit on all flesh did not regenerate flesh or renew the minds of those who walked in incredible gifting. Stated plainly, *a person can prophesy and be profoundly accurate, but that does not speak to their character or the weakness of their unregenerated flesh. A person can have the most amazing healing gift, but that does not speak to their character or the weakness of their unregenerated flesh.* The gifts of the Spirit *are gifts* and work whether we have character or not, they are *gifts* from God given for His purposes. The gifts of the Spirit do not mean that God is affirming our doctrine or our lifestyles; *they are gifts*. Just because someone gives me a car does not mean I am a great driver or that my driving practices are perfect. It means someone gifted me a car and I can use it however I choose, regardless of how many laws I break.

That is why they are the lesser works; they are gifts that are poured out on *unregenerate flesh with fallen genetics and unrenewed minds.* They work regardless of the character of the one possessing the gifts. I do not say this to disrespect those named above or other unnamed generals; I honor and respect them greatly. I say this only to contrast anointed vulnerable flesh with the coming greater works.

With the passing of the last generation of Kingdom generals, I believe God has released a move towards the greater works. God wants us to move beyond where they were, not repeat the level of gifting they walked in. *He is not interested in anyone picking up mantles from the past.* He wants us to walk in what He desires for this generation, not a repeat of past generations. I cannot say enough that I honor those who have gone before us to pave the way, to show us the awe and wonder of the love of God through the lesser works. But I choose not to remain in the level of gifting they demonstrated.

I am not looking to be the next Smith Wigglesworth or Oral Roberts. I am looking to step into the greater works. I am looking to launch from the highest heights of the developed lesser works demonstrated by those with a love and passion for Christ and for the lost.

Before we get into the greater works, let's look at what Jesus said to clearly define the lesser works.

> Most assuredly, I say to you, he who believes in Me, *the works that I do he will do also*, and *greater works* than these he will do, because I go to My Father.
> John 14:12 (emphasis added)

What an incredible statement. *We are to do the works of Jesus and even greater.* I know it is hard to fathom for some, but they are in fact the words of Jesus. We either believe what Jesus said or we do not. The choice to believe Him is ours to make; no one else can make it for us. Theologians cannot make it for us. Commentaries cannot make it for us; university professors cannot make it for us, and spiritual leaders cannot make it for us. People are not the source of our salvation. While we can and must learn from others, others cannot make the decision to believe for us. We must make the decision to believe ourselves.

7 : THE LESSER WORKS

Jesus said we would do what He did and greater. He also said the greater would come because He was going to His Father. *Jesus made it clear the greater works would not come or be seen until He left the earth and went to His Father.* That means Jesus classified everything we saw Him do before His ascension back to the Father as a lesser work in comparison to what was coming. *By His own admission, Jesus did not work the greater works; He worked only the lesser works.*

We can choose to minimize what Jesus said by saying something like, "Oh, He meant greater in quantity, He could not have meant greater in the sense of the miraculous." "Oh, He meant salvation was greater than the miracles He did." "Oh, who could do greater things than Jesus did?" "Clearly, we can't do anything greater than Jesus did." If we believe that, then we are marginalizing the reality and truth of what Jesus Himself said is coming.

Let's revisit what Jesus said. In verse 12, Jesus said, "He who *believes in Me.*" That means our faith and belief in Jesus is necessary to do what He said we would do — *both the lesser and the greater works require faith.* Second, Jesus said we would do the works that He did. That means if we saw Him do it in scripture, then those who believe in Him would do it also. If you saw Jesus do it, it is His intent that we do it today as an ongoing expression of the lesser works. Here is a list of some of the things Jesus did:

> Turned water into wine, walked on water, passed through crowds unseen and untouched, opened blind eyes, caused the lame to walk, read the hearts of men, fed the multitudes, forgave sins, raised the dead, translated a boat full of disciples across the water in an instant, and stood transfigured with Moses and Elijah in front of Peter, James, and John.

For us to work the lesser works Jesus worked, we must understand how He did them. Jesus did the works He did by the anointing of Holy Spirit. One day while in the Synagogue, Jesus read from Isaiah 61:1-2.

> "The Spirit of the Lord is upon Me, because *He has anointed Me*
> to preach the gospel to the poor; He has sent Me to heal the brokenhearted,
> to proclaim liberty to the captives and recovery of sight to the blind,
> to set at liberty those who are oppressed;
> to proclaim the acceptable year of the Lord."
> Luke 4:18-19 (emphasis added)

Jesus said the Spirit of the Lord was upon Him and that He was anointed. After He read that passage, He said the scripture was fulfilled in their hearing that day. *God poured His Spirit out on Jesus.* Luke the writer of the Book of Acts further supports Jesus being anointed by God.

> ...how God *anointed Jesus of Nazareth with the Holy Spirit and power*, who went about doing good and healing all who were oppressed by the devil, *for God was with Him.*
> Acts 10:38 (emphasis added)

It is abundantly clear that Jesus operated by the anointing of Holy Spirit. To do the works Jesus classified as lesser, we must operate the same way He did – by the anointing of Holy Spirit. There is ample scripture to demonstrate this truth.

> Behold, I send the Promise of My Father upon you; but tarry in the city of Jerusalem until you are endued with *power* from on high.
> Luke 24:49 (emphasis added)

> He who believes and is baptized will be saved; but he who does not believe will be condemned. *And these signs will follow those who believe*: In My name, they will cast out demons; they will speak with new tongues; they will take up serpents; and if they drink anything deadly, it will by no means hurt them; they will lay hands on the sick, and they will recover.
> Mark 16:16-18 (emphasis added)

> ...the Spirit of truth, whom the world cannot receive because it neither sees Him nor knows Him; but you know Him, *for He dwells with you and will be in you.*
> John 14:17 (emphasis added)

Jesus sent Holy Spirit to empower us the way Holy Spirit empowered Him. Now, let's look at Jesus and the gifts of the Spirit. Paul outlined the nine gifts of the Spirit in 1 Corinthians 12:8-11: The word of wisdom, the word of knowledge, faith, gifts of healings, the working of miracles, prophecy, discerning of spirits, different kinds of tongues and interpretation of tongues. The easiest thing for us to do is to say, "He did it because He was the Son of God." But that is not what Jesus said, He said Holy Spirit anointed Him. He did

7 : THE LESSER WORKS

what He did by the anointing of Holy Spirit, not because of who He was as God. Philippians 2:5-8, makes it very clear that Jesus emptied Himself when He took on the form of man.

> Let this mind be in you which was also in Christ Jesus, *who, being in the form of God*, did not consider it robbery to be equal with God, but made Himself of *no reputation*, taking the form of a bondservant, and coming in the likeness of men. And being found in appearance as a man, *He humbled Himself and became obedient to the point of death, even the death of the cross.* (emphasis added)

This book is not intended to be an academic work, but a clear and simple approach to reveal the reality of our redemption and destiny as believers. But there is something we must view from a theological and academic perspective. Paul said Jesus was in the form of God and equal with God. He also said He "*made Himself of no reputation.*" Theologians commonly refer to this event as the "kenosis." The kenosis is a *self-emptying or voiding*. Jesus emptied Himself of who He was as God, while in the form of God, to come into the earth in the likeness, appearance, and form of man.

Paul said Jesus was in the form of, and equal with God. It is important to note that Paul did not say Jesus abandoned His form. He said He *emptied His form* and came in the form of man. When you empty a cup, the cup does not cease to exist; the empty cup is still capable of receiving whatever it previously contained. That is the case with Jesus. The first question is, what is the form of God? I believe Jesus Himself answered that question.

> *God is Spirit*, and those who worship Him must worship in spirit and truth.
> John 4:24 (emphasis added)

Jesus said God is Spirit. That, I believe, is the form of God. So, when Jesus descended, He emptied Himself but retained His form as God, *as Spirit*, and descended to fill the form of man with the emptied form of God.

While it is debatable as to what Jesus specifically emptied Himself of, there are two things that are very clear. He left heaven in the form of God to inhabit the form of man, and He remained in that humbled state all the way through His death, burial, resurrection, and ascension. Yet, the question remains, "What did He empty Himself of?" I believe He emptied

Himself of *His divine attributes of omnipotence, omniscience, and omnipresence, and His role defined, interdependent relationship with the other two members of the Godhead.*

I believe Jesus retained His divine nature as the form of God, but emptied the form so He could not operate out of it independent of the other two members of the Godhead and the gifts of the Spirit. What does that mean? It means that in their unified relationship, the Father does what the Father does, the Son does what the Son does, and Holy Spirit does what Holy Spirit does. It means when Jesus emptied Himself, He emptied Himself of His divine attributes and His unified relationship with the other two members of the Godhead. The level of oneness and unity He had with them was severed at His incarnation and could only be realized through Spirit baptism and obedient union with them while on earth.

> When He had been baptized, Jesus came up immediately from the water, and behold, the heavens were opened to Him, and He saw the Spirit of God descending like a dove and alighting upon Him.
> Matthew 3:16

When Jesus was baptized in the Holy Spirit, *it was a family reunion.* That reunion filled the emptied form of God in Jesus of Nazareth with the Father He was equal to prior to His incarnation. That is why Jesus said, "*It is my Father in Me who does the works*" and "*If you've seen Me, you've seen the Father*" (John 14:9-10). The Father filled the emptied form of God in Christ.

When Jesus the Son of God, in the emptied form of God, descended to inhabit the form of man, He merged the form of God with the form of man. As we said a moment ago, when you empty a cup, the cup can be refilled with what it formerly contained. By placing the form of God in the form of man, He made the form of man capable of receiving the nature, attributes, characteristics, and fullness of God.

Another question to be asked, "When Jesus emptied Himself, where did He leave the emptied contents of His form?" If all things are in Christ, what is big enough to contain what He emptied Himself of? The answer, I believe, is very simple. He left Himself in His Father. John's Gospel confirms this as truth: "*No one has seen God at any time. The only-begotten Son, who is in the bosom of the Father, He has declared Him*" (John 1:18). By leaving Himself in His Father, the only way Jesus could gain access to fill the form of God

7 : THE LESSER WORKS

Spirit He emptied was to go deep into the place He left Himself — back into His Father. Jesus was in His Father and therefore gained access, through obedient relational unity, to all He emptied Himself of.

When we are born from above, we are new creatures in Christ capable of things we were not formerly capable of. We become much more than the first Adam. We are now born of spirit, *which is the very form of God.* Christ can now be formed in us the way the fullness of the Godhead inhabited the emptied form of God in Christ (Colossians 2:9). What happened when we were born from above, when we became a new creature in Christ? God placed the form of God in the form of man so He could personally inhabit the form of God within the form of man, just like He did with Jesus. That is the release point for the fullness of the image and likeness of God into our whole being.

As we said a moment ago, Christ's baptism was a family reunion. It is important to notice that when Jesus was baptized, the heavens were opened to Him. That is a very significant statement and part of our redemption. We often think of a poor, emaciated Jesus dragging Himself across the rocks to be tempted by the devil during His 40-days of fasting. That is not what the Bible says. It says the heavens were opened to Him and then in Matthew 4:2, it says that *afterward,* He was hungry.

Jesus went into the wilderness. When He did, He ascended through prayer into the heavens that were opened to Him to be reunited with His Father. While in the heavens, He received His Father's vision so it would be on earth as it is in heaven through His surrendered life and ministry, and through His ongoing relational unity and obedience to His Father by the Spirit. The reality is that when Jesus *ascended to heaven* in the wilderness, He did not return to earth relationally. He remained united with His Father — in the bosom of His Father - the same way we are seated in heavenly places in Christ Jesus (John 1:18).

> No one has *ascended to heaven* but He who came *down from heaven,* that is, the Son of Man who *is in heaven.*
> John 3:13 (emphasis added)

Jesus made it clear that He came down *from heaven,* ascended back *to heaven,* and was currently *in heaven.* His earthly life was completely surrendered to His heavenly existence in His Father so He could say things like, "*He who has seen Me has seen the Father*" (John 14:9). Jesus lived in two places at once with an awareness of both: in the earth as man and the heavens in His Father. He then operated in obedience through the gifts of the Spirit to carry out what He saw His Father doing. Satan knew that. That is why he crafted the temptations *in the earth* to direct Jesus' attention *to the earth* and away from the direction He received from His Father *in heaven*.

Jesus spent 40-days with His Father like Moses spent 40-days on the mountain. Afterward, Satan came to tempt Him (Matthew 4:1-11). Though Satan tempted Jesus, He remained without sin (Hebrews 4:15). While the temptations are multifaceted, it is interesting to note two common themes. First, the temptations took place *on earth*; therefore, if Jesus had yielded to the temptations He would have received His direction *on earth* from someone *on earth* and not from His Father *in heaven*. Jesus made it clear that He did not do anything unless He saw His Father, *in heaven*, do it. Though He operated by the gifts, He only used the gifts to do what He saw His Father *in heaven* do (John 5:19-20).

Secondly, all three temptations required Jesus to look *down*. "Turn the stones into bread." Where do you look to find a stone? You look *down*. Then, "Cast yourself *down*, and, bow *down*." Satan wanted Jesus to fall from His heavenly place in the Father and back to the earth. *Jesus refused to act based on what He saw and heard on earth.* God does not want us to use Kingdom power and authority to modify the earth based on what we see and hear on earth. He wants it to be *on earth as it is in heaven*.

With the understanding that Jesus ascended back into unified relationship with His Father and operated by the anointing and the gifts of the Spirit, let's take a minute to look at the gifts as they relate to the attributes of God.

I believe the gifts of the Spirit are the attributes of God necessarily modified to find expression through yielded humanity with fallen genetics. Even though Jesus did not operate out of fallen genetics and had the Spirit without measure, He clearly limited Himself to operate by the anointing and gifts of the Spirit. The Father, who was with and in Jesus, found expression through Jesus by way of the gifts of the Spirit (John 3:33-35; Acts 10:38). When we compare the gifts of the Spirit to the attributes of God in the life of Christ, we will see an amazing parallel.

7 : THE LESSER WORKS

Many theologians advocate a 3-3-3 categorical breakdown of the nine gifts. They categorize them as the *power gifts*: faith, healings, miracles; the *revelation gifts*: wisdom, knowledge and discernment; and the *utterance gifts*: tongues, interpretation of tongues, and prophecy. I believe a breakdown of these gifts strongly parallels the attributes of God. The attributes of God are omnipotence (all-powerful — the power gifts), omniscience (all-knowing — the revelation gifts), and omnipresence (everywhere present — the utterance gifts).

How interesting. *The power gifts* of faith, healings, and miracles are a modified expression of the *omnipotence* of God. *The revelation gifts* are a modified expression of the *omniscience* of God, and *the utterance gifts* are a modified expression of the *omnipresence* of God. While the power gifts and the revelation gifts are more obvious expressions of God's omnipotence and omniscience, some may question how the utterance gifts are an expression of God's omnipresence.

In Matthew 8:5-13, Jesus had a conversation with a Centurion. The Centurion asked Jesus to heal his servant. Jesus said He would go to the Centurion's home, but the Centurion told Jesus that all He had to do was speak the word and his servant would be healed. Jesus spoke the word and the Centurion's servant was healed that same hour. Though Jesus did not physically go to the Centurion's home, *He spoke, and His word (His utterance)* went to the Centurion's home and healed the servant. By speaking, it was as if He was in both places at once; a modified expression of omnipresence while incarnate.

Jesus worked the lesser works by the gifts of the Spirit while in unified relationship with His Father and Holy Spirit. Those gifts expressed the attributes of God. That is also how we are to walk in the lesser works; by the gifts of the Spirit while in unified relationship with our Father, with Jesus, and with Holy Spirit.

The lesser works have not gone away, but Jesus did not stop at the lesser works in John 14:12. He said we would not only do the works He did, but even greater works. *God is interested in moving beyond the anointing of flesh to the restoration of flesh into full sonship.* He wants to restore our flesh — to become the incarnate body of Christ — to the point that the form of God in us can be made one with our restored genetics to reveal the fullness of the Godhead. The Father wants to reveal Himself through us as *new creatures* in spiritual union with Christ to reveal the fullness of the Godhead in, to, and through man.

7 : THE LESSER WORKS

CHAPTER 8:
THE GREATER WORKS

I believe the greater works go beyond God pouring out of His Spirit upon flesh. The greater works are the transformation of humanity and fallen genetics through the blood of Jesus, the incorruptible seed that is the Word of God, the Law of the Spirit of life in Christ, as the body of Christ, and the same Spirit that raised Christ from the dead. Together, they bring the full image and likeness of God into the creation through us.

Jesus humbled Himself to work only the lesser works. Jesus, in His self-appointed humility, could not reveal His true nature and identity as God. He intentionally operated as the anointed Son of Man rather than the heavenly Son of God. He kept His Sonship and true nature veiled to operate only in the lesser works by the anointing of Holy Spirit. As sons, *we are called to reveal what Jesus had to keep veiled. He was the Son of God who did not manifest so we could be manifest sons of God.* We are to operate out of who we are as sons of God with and as the body of Christ, rather than solely by the anointing and gifts of the Spirit given to the sons of men.

The elements for our full redemption are already in us. The blood of Jesus as the genesis of our genetic redemption *is in us*, the incorruptible seed that is the Word of God *is in us*, the law of the Spirit of life in Christ as the body of Christ, *is in us*, and the same Spirit that raised Christ from the dead *is in us*. We have all we need. These elements are not contained in a time-released capsule awaiting the catching away of the church. They are in a faith-released capsule awaiting our agreement; waiting for us to believe for our full redemption now.

We said this earlier: "When we are born from above, we are a new creation in Christ capable of things we were not formerly capable of. We become much more than the first Adam. God has created us so that internally we are spirit, *which is the very form of God.* Christ can now be formed in us the way the fullness of the Godhead inhabited the emptied form of God in Christ (Colossians 2:9). What happened when we were born from above, when we became a new creation in Christ? God placed the form of God in the form of man so He could personally inhabit the form of God within the form of man, just like He did with Jesus. That is the release point for the fullness of the image and likeness of God into our whole being. That is why Christ came." *God living in us as the body of Christ should have greater meaning than going to heaven one day, His indwelling presence should impact our whole being and the world around us.*

Before the fall, Adam could bear and release the image of God as a living soul in relationship with God. Adam's unfallen genetics and living soul partnered to release the image and ever-increasing likeness of God he encountered in his ongoing relationship with God. Adam was constantly being transformed as the genetic structures of his body took on the likeness of God that he observed in his encounters with Him. When he encountered God, he beheld as in a mirror the glory of the Lord and was transformed into that image from glory to glory. Our fallen genetics are not capable of a full and complete merger with the form of God within us. We cannot truly be whole as a person when our body cannot fully merge with our born from above, new creation spirit. The reason the works are greater is that God is not merely pouring His Spirit out *on our flesh*, He is pouring His Spirit out *through our flesh as Christ's body, through our whole restored being.*

The greater works are the release of all God is in us, in partnership with renewed minds and our transmutation from the body of the first Adam into the body of Christ. Our fallen bodies are not capable of being one with the form of God; that is why Jesus told us to receive His body and His blood through communion to have eternal life. In truth, that is what the new wineskin is, it is our regenerated, transmuted body. Spirit is not the new wineskin, spirit is the new wine of God living on the inside of us. It is the old body that is

8 : THE GREATER WORKS

the old wineskin. That body cannot fully express the new wine of the spirit, the Godhead in man (Matthew 9:17). Through communion, God has deposited the body and the blood of Jesus in us. We are the *resurrected body of Christ* with the ability to genetically bear His image. Every encounter we have with God comes with the divine potential to encode itself in our very genome. Now we, beholding as in a mirror, are being transformed from glory to glory to bear the *encoded image of God in our DNA* (2 Corinthians 3:18).

Communion changes our bodies to enable us to receive and release the image and likeness of God from within — it is a genetic alchemy. Our fallen genetics in their current form are not the proper conduit for the flow of God; that is why we need the gifts of the Spirit to anoint our sons of men's flesh. When we receive communion, it is a release of Christ's body and blood in us. Christ's body and blood become the faith-based genetic structure in our bodies so God can be released through us, not just on us. Whether you believe we receive the actual body and blood of Jesus or that it is imputed to us by faith like Abraham received righteousness, the result is the same (Genesis 15:6). God can reveal Himself in, to, and through us.

That is the whole reason for this book. It is to help renew our minds to understand all God has made available now, through the merger of God and man, and God as man. As we will discuss in Chapter 12, God did not make the saints of old wait for the cross to benefit from Christ's death, burial, and resurrection. Likewise, God is not making us wait on the catching away of the church to receive the full benefit of redemption and all it means. Faith brings the fruit of future events into our lives now. *Time is not our master.*

Jesus said we would do the greater works because He was going to His Father. *To work the greater works is to do greater works than both the first and Last Adams.* Because Jesus in His self-appointed humility could not reveal His true nature as the Son of God, we are called and empowered to reveal more of Christ than Christ revealed of Himself. We are called to reveal more of the Father than Christ could reveal of the Father in His self-appointed humility as the Son of Man. When Jesus returned to His Father, He sent Holy Spirit to facilitate our relationship with God and the transformation of our whole being resulting in the greater works He was not allowed to walk in.

> ...the Spirit of truth, whom the world cannot receive
> because it neither sees Him nor knows Him; but you know Him,
> *for He dwells with you and will be in you.*
> John 14:17 (emphasis added)

> At that day, you will know that *I am in My Father, and you in Me, and I in you.* He who *has My commandments and keeps them*, it is he who loves Me. And he who loves Me will be loved by My Father, and I will love him *and manifest Myself to him.*
> John 14:20-21 (emphasis added)

In these scriptures, Jesus made three things very clear: 1. He said He would send Holy Spirit (the Spirit of Truth) who was with them, to be in them (and us), 2. We would know that He is in His Father; we are in Him, and He in us, and 3. He would manifest (*disclose and reveal*) Himself to those who keep His commandants and love Him.

Just like God filled the form of God in Christ with the Godhead, Christ has filled the new creation form of God in man with the Godhead. If you question or do not believe that, let's review the scriptures we just read.

> "...the Spirit of truth, whom the world cannot receive
> because it neither sees Him nor knows Him; but you know Him,
> *for He dwells with you and will be in you.*
> John 14:17 (emphasis added)

> At that day, you will know that *I am in My Father, and you in Me, and I in you.* He who *has My commandments and keeps them*, it is he who loves Me. And he who loves Me will be loved by My Father, and I will love Him *and manifest Myself to him.*
> John 14:20-21 (emphasis added)

These two scriptures make it abundantly clear that both Holy Spirit and Christ live in the believer. Furthermore, the Father is in Christ and Christ is in the Father, which means both the Father and the Son are in us and we are in them. That unified relationship is the merger of God and man, *the Godhead in man, and man in the Godhead.* We must get over our "woe is me" thinking and recognize the value God placed on humanity. He became sin

8 : THE GREATER WORKS

and experienced death, burial, and the resurrection on our behalf; that should be a hint!

The next question is, "How does this relational dynamic of the Godhead in the believer result in the greater works when Jesus had that same relationship and only walked in the lesser works?" We will get to that in a moment. Let's revisit what Paul said in the Book of Philippians first.

> Let this mind be in you which was also in Christ Jesus, who, *being in the form of God*, did not consider it robbery to be equal with God, *but made Himself of no reputation, taking the form of a bondservant, and coming in the likeness of men. And being found in appearance as a man, He humbled Himself and became obedient to the point of death, even the death of the cross.*
> Philippians 2:5-8 (emphasis added)

We looked at this passage of scripture earlier when we discussed the kenosis, so we do not need to cover that again. In this passage, Paul made it clear that Jesus left heaven and came in the form of a bondservant and the likeness of men. He further stated that Jesus humbled Himself and *remained in that humbled state all the way through His death on the cross.*

Stated simply, *Jesus did not reveal the form of God while in the form of man.* He remained humbled and in the form and appearance of a man even though He was filled with the fullness of the Godhead. Jesus did not and would not reveal the reality or fullness of who He was or who was in Him while He was on the earth. Therefore, He operated as the anointed Son of Man by the gifts of the Spirit as the lesser works, and not out of His true nature as the Son of God who was filled with the fullness of the Godhead bodily.

Israel was no stranger to miracles. Moses and the prophets were anointed and worked many miracles in God's history with them. Miracles were not considered evidence that someone was God; they were considered evidence that God was with the person performing the miracles. That is why Luke said, *"God was with Him"* (Acts 10:38); God was with Jesus. That is also why Nicodemus said, "Rabbi, we know that you are a teacher come from God; for no one can do these signs that you do unless *God is with him*" (John 3:1). *God was with*

Jesus. Now let's look at what Paul said to confirm Jesus did not reveal His true nature as God's Son.

> But we speak the wisdom of God in a mystery, the hidden wisdom which God ordained for our glory, which none of the rulers of this age knew; *for had they known, they would not have crucified the Lord of glory.* But as it is written: Eye has not seen, nor ear heard, nor have entered into the heart of man the things which God has prepared for those who love Him. But God has revealed them to us through His Spirit. For the Spirit searches all things, yes, the deep things of God.
> 1 Corinthians 2:7-10 (Emphasis added)

These verses are incredibly important, Paul said six things: 1. He spoke the wisdom of God in a mystery, 2. That wisdom was hidden, 3. The hidden wisdom was ordained for our glory, 4. The rulers of this age did not know the hidden wisdom of that mystery, 5. If they had known, they would not have crucified Jesus; the Lord of glory, and, 6. The Spirit of God would reveal that hidden wisdom to us.

Let's begin by stating the not so obvious. The mystery that was reserved by God for our glory was not revealed through Jesus. That wisdom was hidden *in Christ* to be revealed to us and through us as the greater works by the Spirit of God after Christ's ascension.

How do we know that Jesus did not reveal that hidden wisdom? First, because Paul said it was ordained for our glory, not Christ's. Second, *when speaking of that mystery,* Paul said eye has not seen, nor ear heard, nor had it entered the heart of man the things which God has prepared for those who love Him. Jesus had already been in the earth and ascended to heaven by the time Paul wrote this. The works of Jesus were seen by eyes, heard by ears, and entered the heart of man. Because the things Jesus said and did in His earthly ministry entered the heart of man, the lesser works He demonstrated *were not the mystery ordained for our glory.*

Jesus Himself considered His works in the earth, the lesser works. That includes by the way, Jesus, Moses, and Elijah on the Mount of Transfiguration. Peter, James, and John saw and heard it and it entered their hearts. So even the transfiguration of Jesus was a lesser work.

8 : THE GREATER WORKS

Paul said it would be Holy Spirit that revealed the hidden mystery; therefore, Jesus could not reveal it and remain within the will of His Father. There are four basic reasons Jesus did not reveal the hidden mystery: 1. It was ordained for our glory; not His, 2. They would not have killed Him if He had, 3. It was not His purpose to reveal it, that role belongs to the Spirit of God in the believer, 4. Jesus was to return to the glory He had with His Father before the world was created, not walk in the glory destined for us (John 17:5).

While it is hard for us to imagine that Jesus remained humble to operate only in the lesser works, it is true. Since eyes did not see it, ears did not hear it, and it did not enter the heart of man from Jesus, it means Jesus did not reveal it through the "lesser" works He performed in the earth. Those works were not the mystery; they did not represent the glory of the hidden wisdom Paul was talking about.

Jesus said we would do the greater works, when He did, He was focused on our impending unified relationship with the Godhead in us as the source of the coming greater works. Jesus willfully chose to reserve the greater works, as the hidden mystery, for the glory of those who love Him. Jesus focused on God's impending unified relationship with man as the source of the greater works, and Paul focused on the Spirit of God's role to reveal the hidden wisdom to and through those who love God.

Let's break this down very simply. Jesus left heaven in the form of God to inhabit the form of man. He then worked the lesser works by the anointing of Holy Spirit as the Son of Man and remained humble all the way through to His death, burial, resurrection, and ascension. Then Paul said there was a mystery that was ordained for our glory and if the rulers of this age had known that *hidden mystery*, they would not have killed Jesus. He also said that eyes had not seen, ears had not heard, and it had not entered the heart of man those things (*the hidden mystery*) that God has prepared for those who love Him.

What is the bottom line of the mystery? The mystery is God in man fully revealing the image *and* likeness of God. It is the return to a pre-fall construct and beyond, through our spiritual union with Christ, and our corresponding ascension into the heavens, in and as the body of Christ. It is not God blessing or anointing the fallen condition of mankind by merely pouring out His Spirit upon all flesh as before — Old Testament saints experienced that. It is not carnal, but spiritually redeemed humanity operating under the anointing with the gifts of the Spirit while abiding under the shadow of death. That is the lesser work. The greater work is the visible, tangible, and authoritative restoration of the pre-fall condition of mankind, and beyond, through the blood of Jesus and our relationship with God. It is the relationship that came because Jesus remained humbled, then returned to His Father to allow the fullness of the Godhead to abide in man to be revealed through man. That is the mystery and revelation of the greater works.

The fullness of the Godhead was in Jesus, *but He was not allowed to reveal the fullness of His identity as the Son of God for the world to see.* If He had, they would not have crucified Him. He intentionally operated by the anointing and the gifts of the Spirit to walk in the lesser works demonstrating God was with Him, not demonstrating He was God (Luke 4:18-19; Acts 10:38). Think about it, what God-fearing man or nation would kill God if they knew the person they were killing was God?

Let's ask the question one more time. "What are the greater works?" As we said at the beginning of this chapter, the greater works are simply this: "*As sons, we are called to reveal what Jesus had to keep veiled. Jesus was the Son of God who did not manifest so we could be manifest sons of God!*"

To further clarify, the greater works are not merely that God our Father, Jesus and Holy Spirit live in us. That is the same relationship Jesus had when He walked the earth and that is not a greater work. The greater work is that we get to fully reveal who lives in us because Jesus in His self-appointed humility could not allow it to be seen visibly through His spirit, soul, or body. Jesus could not reveal anything that would prevent His death. If He had, they would not have crucified Him and we would not be redeemed through His work on the cross.

Now, today, the Spirit of God searches the deep things of God in our form of God spirit and DNA to reveal and form Christ in us as the greater works. The greater works are the transformation of humanity and fallen genetics through the blood of Jesus, the incorruptible seed that is the Word of God, the Law of the Spirit of life in Christ as the body of Christ, and the same Spirit that raised Christ from the dead. Together, they bring the full image and likeness of God into the creation through us as we are transfigured from the image of the first Adam into the image of Last Adam. That is the manifestation of the

8 : THE GREATER WORKS

greater works and fully revealed sonship. God lives in us to transform and transfigure us from the image and body of the fallen first Adam into the image and body of the risen Last Adam. We are to bear the image and full expression of the Godhead as new creation beings in spiritual union with Christ.

> We are called to visibly and dynamically release the previously hidden mystery: God fully revealed in, to, and through man, as fully revealed and manifest sonship.

The lesser works are the things Jesus did by the anointing and gifts of Holy Spirit operating in His life — He limited Himself to the lesser works as the anointed Son of Man. The greater works are who He redeemed us to be: fully revealed manifest sons of our Father in heaven. The lesser works are *what we continue to do by the anointing and gifts of the Spirit* and the greater works are *who we are* and *who we ultimately reveal through our redemption to full sonship*. God anointing sons of men on earth is the lesser work. God transforming us into the body of Christ to reveal who we are in Christ, and who Christ is in us, on earth, is the greater work. God anointing our lives to do the works Jesus did will always be the lesser, God revealing the Godhead and His true nature through us will always be the greater. The greater work is not merely about what we do, it is about who we are and who we mature to reveal — it is revealing the full image and likeness of God through our being without measure. The lesser works are doing, the greater works are being and releasing the full nature of God back into the creation.

We are called to fully express and reveal to eyes, ears, and hearts throughout the creation the mystery that God lives in complete union with man. Eyes can now see it, ears can now hear it, it can now enter the hearts of men. All because Jesus shed His blood, ascended to His Father and sent Holy Spirit to conform us to His image from glory to glory — *the very glory* that was the mystery of the hidden wisdom ordained *for our glory*; God in humanity revealed in His fullness.

We are called to the greater work of fully revealing the Father and the Son to the creation and those in it. The first Adam did not have the spiritual capacity - God did not live in the first Adam — and Jesus in His self-appointed humility, would not. We are called to mature from glory to glory until we are fully transformed into the image, the likeness, and the transfigured incarnate expression of God in Christ and Christ in us. That is the fullness of our transformation into sons of God: spirit, soul and body. Mystery revealed. It is restoration to full sonship beyond the first Adam into our very existence as manifest sons of God. We are sons of our Father, who is light. That makes us sons of light who release the light that is God Himself.

Simply stated, with finality, Jesus was not allowed to reveal that mystery; He secured our redemption so we could reveal it. *That is our job.* He came as the Last Adam to impart and release the image and likeness of God in man so His original plan for mankind could be realized. Now the mystery is revealed, it is God that needs to be fully and completely revealed through restored and glorified sons of light in the heavens and the earth. Jesus, the light of the world filled with the glory of His Father could not reveal it. God gave us that very same glory and light and He has called us to be fully transfigured into His image and likeness so we can fully reveal what Jesus had to keep veiled. *That is the greater work!*

8 : THE GREATER WORKS

CHAPTER 9: OVERCOMING TO REIGN

Jesus said, "To him who overcomes, I will grant to sit with Me on my throne, as I also overcame and sat with My Father on His throne" (Revelation 3:11). What does it mean to overcome? As we said in a previous chapter, "To overcome is to reject the iniquitous genetic history and record passed down from our parents in favor of God's incorruptible seed that is the Word of God — just like Jesus overcame by rejecting the fallen genetics from Mary. It means we reject the old and all that is from our former fallen nature and self-image to embrace what God has done for us and who He is in us, so we can reveal His image, thoughts, and ways to the creation." Jesus said He overcame, but how do we overcome? We have conversations with God.

> "There's no greater lifestyle and no greater happiness than that of having a continual conversation with God." Brother Lawrence[5]

What is a conversation? A conversation is an exchange of illuminations between two parties. If I were to say to you, "I'm lost, how do I get to the interstate from here?" If you knew how to get to the interstate, or the motorway if you are one of my friends in the United Kingdom, you would respond by giving me directions.

---

5   www.inspiringquotes.us/author/9767-brother-lawrence

The point here is that my question illuminates a response within you. You would not respond by telling me where you bought your shoes or where you bought your groceries. That is not what I asked. You would respond based on my question. That is exactly how it works with God. Psalm 119:130 says, "The entrance of God's Word gives light." Light illuminates. What does God's Word illuminate? His Word illuminates and generates a response within us. Let's look at Isaiah 55, and later, Matthew 4, as proof texts to highlight this truth.

> Seek the Lord while He may be found; call upon Him while He is near. *Let the wicked forsake their ways and the unrighteous their thoughts.* Let them turn to the Lord, and He will have mercy on them, and to our God, for He will freely pardon. For My thoughts are not your thoughts, neither are your ways My ways, declares the Lord. *As the rain and the snow come down from heaven,* and do not return to it without watering the earth and making it bud and flourish, so that it yields seed for the sower and bread for the eater, *so is My word that goes out from My mouth*: It will not return to Me empty, but will accomplish what I desire and achieve the purpose for which I sent it.
> Isaiah 55:6-8 (emphasis added)

We were born into an unrighteous and wicked world. We have thought countless unrighteous thoughts and have observed countless wicked ways that are considered normal today. They are a part of daily life in the earth and serve to form our worldview, belief systems, and way of life. By default, we have developed a thought life and lifestyle patterned after the basic principles of the world. We do not have to be overtly wicked or unrighteous on earth to have ways and thoughts that are inconsistent with God's thoughts and ways in heaven. That is the point of all of this.

By default, we think according to what we have heard and learned on earth rather than what God thinks in heaven. That is why He sent His Word from heaven, just like the rain and the snow, to produce a harvest in us consist with His thoughts and ways. When God's thoughts enter our hearts through His Word and through our conversations with Him, they illuminate a response from what is already in our hearts.

We have heard preacher after preacher preach against every other preacher. Which one is right? Do we know which doctrinal view is correct? Do we know which of the preacher's

9 : OVERCOMING TO REIGN

thoughts are God's thoughts, and which thoughts are his or her own, or the thoughts of a denomination? One preacher says the gifts of the Spirit are for today; another says the gifts of the Spirit ceased when the last original apostle died. Is my pastor right, or is your pastor right? In fact, am I right in what I believe, are you right in what you believe? There are tens of thousands of religious organizations in Christendom that rally around their own understanding of who God is and what He is, or is not doing today. They cannot all be right. Let's be honest, we tend to believe whatever we have been taught by the Christian community we are from. That is not hearing from God; that is hearing from man.

At some point, all of us have believed and shared something that was not consistent with God's thoughts or ways. I do not know about you, but while my foundational doctrines of Christ have not changed, many of my other views have changed because of increased revelation in my relationship with God. I believe differently today than I did five years ago because I have matured through conversations with God. And chances are, I will believe differently in five years than I believe now. If I do not, then I have not grown in my relationship with God. God does not reveal the fullness of who He is in one encounter; He reveals more and more of Himself as we engage in ongoing, deeper relationship with Him. Our lives should be an ongoing conversation wherein God reveals more and more of Himself to us as our daily bread.

I was in the United States Army from early 1977 through late 1987. While in the Army, I was a helicopter pilot; I flew OH-58 Kiowas, UH-1 Hueys and UH-60 Blackhawk helicopters. A Blackhawk helicopter is a Sikorsky product. On one occasion, I picked up a Blackhawk from the Sikorsky factory in Stratford, Connecticut. The other pilot and I flew from Connecticut to Fort Lewis, Washington. We flew from one coast to the other over the course of several days. Most of the journey was flying cross-country at a low altitude so we could see things like Mount Rushmore, from a bird's-eye view. On one leg of the journey, however, we had to fly in the clouds with no visual reference to the ground; we were under instrument flight rules (IFR).

That leg of our journey took us over Lake Michigan from east to west to Milwaukee. What is interesting is this: if I flew one degree off course for one minute, it would not really be a problem; but if I flew one degree off course for one hour, I would be nowhere near my intended destination.

The great thing about flying instruments was that I had navigation instruments to tell me if I was on or off course. I had instruments so I could maintain the proper altitude, course, and speed to reach Milwaukee. What is also interesting, is that while flying on instruments, Air Traffic Control (ATC) was communicating with me and giving me instructions. ATC gave me instructions based on things I could not see because I was in the clouds without visual reference to the ground or the airspace around me. It can be like that with God as well. Doctrine is not always a visible thing we can navigate by sight. No one has perfect doctrine; we can all be off by a degree or so and not realize it. Wrong doctrine can affect our spiritual journey, and ultimately, our redemptive destination.

If the navigation instruments in the helicopter were faulty, I would not have known I was off course. I would have thought I was on the correct flight path. If our doctrinal views are faulty, we do not know that we are off course and think we are on the correct spiritual flight path. So, how does God alert us to wrong doctrine, wrong beliefs, wrong thoughts and wrong ways? He has a conversation with us. Just like ATC assisted me on my flight in the clouds, God speaks with us to illuminate things within our hearts to highlight how contrary they are to His thoughts, and ways, to let us know we are off course. As a result, we start to believe differently. Let me give you an example.

In the late 1990's, I was up late at night and into the morning praying in the Spirit. I was praying out the mysteries.

> For he who speaks in an unknown tongue does not speak to men but to God, for no one understands him; however, in the spirit, he speaks mysteries.
> 1 Corinthians 14:2

I was praying and releasing mysteries in the Spirit. It is really important to see that Paul said; *we are not speaking to men, but to God.* When we pray in the Spirit, we are not speaking to men, *we are having a conversation with God.* There are no mysteries to God; He knows everything. The mysteries I am praying are not for Him, they are for me.

When I partner with God to pray in the Spirit, the Spirit of God gives me the utterance (Acts 2:4). Why do I need God to give me the utterance? Because I do not know which of my doctrines or beliefs are consistent with His thoughts and ways. I do not know if I am off

9 : OVERCOMING TO REIGN

course or not, I am guided by what is in my heart. *As he thinks in his heart so is he* (Proverbs 23:7). What is in my heart is not necessarily what is in God's heart. That is why He gave me a language to bypass my intellect and the contents of my heart. As a result, He can reveal the contents of His heart to me through His conversation with me. It is human nature, any information we already know acts as a filter to new information. If you speak to me in a known tongue and tell me something contrary to what I already know and believe, I will reject what you say to me. In fact, it is already happening to some of you as you read this book; what you already know is causing you to reject things that are contrary to what you have been taught and come to believe.

God cannot and will not change us apart from our willful participation with Him. So when we pray in the Spirit, we are using our will to partner with God so He can give us the utterance to work on our behalf. We do not know which of our thoughts are God's thoughts, or which of our thoughts came from man and life in a fallen creation. So God, in His wisdom, gave us a way to pray that partners with our will to intentionally bypass our intellect and the contents of our hearts.

By bypassing our intellect, we do not pray out of the contents of our hearts, we pray by the Spirit as the Spirit of God gives us utterance. The Spirit of God searches the deep things of God concerning us and releases a mystery through the utterance He gives us. When we speak out of that utterance, we are praying mysteries — *things we do not already know.* God hears the mysteries the Spirit is releasing through us because we are speaking directly to Him, not to man. God then answers the mystery we are speaking and responds by depositing His thoughts and His ways in our conscious mind. He does not respond to us in an unknown tongue; He responds by revealing a mystery, a revelation, a sudden knowing or thought to our conscious understanding. That is why Paul said,

> For what man knows the things of man except the spirit of the man which is in him? Even so, no one knows the things of God except the Spirit of God. Now we have received, not the spirit of the world, but the Spirit who is from God, that we might know the things that have been freely given to us by God.
> 2 Corinthians 2:11–12

I summarize that scripture this way: man's spirit knows man's thoughts and ways and God's Spirit knows God's thoughts and ways. So, God gave us His Spirit so we could know His thoughts and ways.

When God's thoughts and ways enter our conscious understanding, it also illuminates any thoughts in our being that are contrary to that particular revelation. That is how conversations work, they illuminate a response consistent with the question asked. We now have a choice, we believe what God said, or we believe the thoughts and feelings that rise from our hearts to exalt themselves against the knowledge of God we just received. This was an experiential revelation for me and was later confirmed by scripture.

As I said, I was up late into the night and early morning intentionally praying in the Spirit. I was praying out mysteries. The room was flooded with the heavy presence of God and He suddenly dropped the most incredible revelation I had ever received. He filled me with a revelation that was then revealed to my conscious mind as a new understanding. When I spoke a mystery to God in tongues, He answered by revealing the mystery to my understanding as a revelation. I prayed the mystery to Him; He revealed the mystery to me.

I was thanking God for what He revealed to me; but within a few moments of receiving the revelation, I began to doubt and reason away what God spoke to my understanding. I suddenly noticed the presence of God had left the room and I felt entirely alone. Not only that, when the presence left, so did the revelation! I was so overtaken by the lack of God's presence and the onslaught of doubt, I literally could not remember what had been up to that point, the greatest revelation of my life.

> The spirit of a man is the lamp of the Lord,
> searching all the inner depths of his heart.
> Proverbs 20:27

I began to repent for the doubt and then asked the Lord a question. I said, "Lord, I know the thief comes immediately for the word's sake, but I have not even spoken what you revealed to me. How did the devil come and get what he didn't know you gave me?" God responded immediately. He said, "Son, the devil isn't within a thousand miles of you. I just let your mind hear your heart's response to the mystery I just revealed to you." Suddenly, the light came on. *The spirit of a man is the lamp of the Lord, searching all the inner depths (or rooms) of his heart.*

When God unlocked a mystery for me in our conversation, He revealed it through my spirit to my understanding. My spirit then became the lamp of the Lord and illuminated the place in my heart that contained what I really believed about what He said to me. The doubts were not the devil, they were deeply held beliefs about God and myself that were resident within my own being. God revealed them to me to give me a choice; I could either believe what He said or hold onto what He revealed was already rooted in my life. He was helping me purify my heart. Going back to my flight over Lake Michigan as an illustration, it was a course correction and I could accept it or reject it – the choice was mine.

Prior to that moment, I always felt condemned because I thought I was doubting God. I thought I did not have enough faith and that I was failing God. So, when God revealed this truth to me, I finally realized I was not doubting God. God is the one who invented this conversational, heart-purifying process. He simply identified the thoughts and ways I was to abandon for His thoughts and ways. I did not realize that receiving a revelation from God actually meant God was having a conversation with me. If we are not actively thinking about God or talking to Him and a sudden revelation drops into our understanding out of nowhere, it means God is either initiating a conversation with us or unlocking a mystery from one of our previous conversations.

God is smart; instead of waiting for me to go on a search and destroy mission to identify which of my beliefs are from Him and which of my beliefs are from man, He used His Word to highlight the very thought in me that was contrary to the revealed mystery He had just given me. God reveals what He wants to change in us by illuminating it for us with His Word. In my case, God shined His Word on the unrighteous thought within me. He needed me to forsake that thought so what He told me could come to pass in my life. It was not me doubting, God was revealing what was in His parking spot in my heart. I learned something new that day; I must choose to reject the argument and accept God's Word. In that experience, God taught me how to overcome one wrong belief system at a time.

Some of you may think the experience I just described reveals how God deals with me rather than how He deals with everyone else, but that is not true. It is the way God reveals and identifies our thoughts and ways to replace them with His thoughts and ways. This truth is evidenced by God's conversation with a young man in the Old Testament; his name is Jeremiah.

> Then the *word of the Lord* came to me, saying: Before I formed you in the womb I knew you; before you were born I sanctified you; I ordained you a prophet to the nations. Then said I: Ah, Lord God! Behold, I cannot speak, for I am a youth. But the Lord said to me: Do not say, 'I am a youth.'
> Jeremiah 1:5-7 (emphasis added)

God initiated a conversation with Jeremiah; God began by revealing a mystery to him. *God told Jeremiah something he did not know prior to that moment.* God told Jeremiah He ordained him a prophet to the nations. God revealed a mystery to Jeremiah the same way He reveals mysteries to us when we pray in the Spirit, with a conversation. The truth is, Jeremiah was just like you and me. His whole system of thought was based on who he was and what he knew up to that point in time.

God spoke to Jeremiah. When He did, He illuminated what was already in Jeremiah's heart. The thoughts in Jeremiah's heart rose up to exalt themselves against the word God had just given him. Jeremiah then spoke and gave voice to those thoughts. "Behold, I cannot speak, for I am a youth." God responded to the argument in Jeremiah's heart and said, "Do not say, 'I am a youth.'" Jeremiah now had a choice to make. He could either *embrace what God said about him* or *retain what he believed about himself* prior to that moment.

That is the process of overcoming. Jeremiah had to overcome the thoughts and ways of his own heart to embrace what God said. When he did, he became the living expression of the mystery God revealed to him; he became a prophet to the nations. It is the conversational process God used with Jeremiah and it is the conversational process God uses with all of us. Let's confirm this with another scripture, this time, the words of Jesus in the context of the parable of the sower.

You are probably familiar with the parable of the sower in Mark 4:1-20. Simply stated, the context of the parable of the sower is the *Word of God* and the *heart of man*. We are not going to focus on the parable itself, we are going to focus on verses 21 and 22 that follow the parable.

9 : OVERCOMING TO REIGN

> Also, He said to them, "Is a lamp brought to be put under a basket or under a bed? Is it not to be set on a lampstand? For there is nothing hidden which will not be revealed, nor has anything been kept secret but that it should come to light."
> Mark 4:21–22

Jesus did not change subjects in verses 21 and 22, He changed illustrations. The context is still the *Word of God* and the *heart of man*. As we said earlier, Psalm 119:130 tells us the entrance of God's Word gives light, and furthermore, Psalm 119:105 says, "Your word is a *lamp* to my feet and a light to my path." There are three specific things to highlight from verses 21 and 22. First, the lamp Jesus is talking about in verse 21 is God's Word, it is what illuminates. Second, the illumination is a revelation. It is a revealed mystery entering the heart of man *with understanding*. If you do not understand something, you cannot retain it. Thirdly, Jesus said there is nothing hidden which would not be revealed and nothing would be kept secret but that it should come to light.

It is really important to notice that Jesus did not say all good things will be revealed and come to light. He said there is *nothing hidden* that will not be revealed, including the hidden thoughts of our hearts which are contrary to His thoughts and His ways. When the Word of God enters our hearts as a revealed mystery, it illuminates everything in the "room" it enters. That is why doubts and fears arise after God has given us a word about our future and the reality of redemption. The Word of God illuminates the doubts and fears for us so we can reject them. God does not illuminate our thoughts to condemn us with them. *He illuminates them so we can eliminate them as they rise to exalt themselves against the knowledge of God.*

This not only applies to doctrine or what we believe about God, it also applies to any and every system of thought we possess, even what we believe about ourselves and others. Everyone has experienced some type of trauma in life; traumas that impact self-image. If we have been told our whole lives that we are unlovable, we will believe that about ourselves. So when someone says, "God loves you" the system of thought within us will immediately argue that we are unlovable. That system of thought exalts itself against the knowledge of God, against the truth that God truly does loves us. We must embrace God's words from heaven, not man's words from the earth, or the belief system already embedded in every fiber of our being.

This is how I have come to deal with everything in my life that argues with God: when opposing thoughts begin to exalt themselves against the knowledge of God, I say, "Thank you, Lord, for showing me the unrighteous thought that needs to leave my heart. I agree with your Word and reject my heart's argument." *What I have just described is spiritual warfare.*

When thoughts and fears arise in our hearts after we receive a word, a mystery, or a revelation from God, it is spiritual warfare. Spiritual warfare you ask? Yes, spiritual warfare. Paul addressed the issue in his second letter to the church at Corinth.

> For though we walk in the flesh, we do not war according to the flesh. For the weapons of our warfare are not carnal but mighty in God for pulling down of *strongholds*, casting down *arguments* and every high thing that exalts itself against *the knowledge of God*, bringing every *thought* into captivity to the obedience of Christ.
> 2 Corinthians 10:3-5 (emphasis added)

That is spiritual warfare. Paul said the weapons of our warfare are not carnal but mighty in God for pulling down of strongholds. I know we tend to think of strongholds as high and lofty things where a principality is seated over a region, but that is not the context of this passage. The context is internal warfare, *arguments* against *the knowledge of God* and *thoughts* that need to be taken captive in obedience to Christ. It is warfare because you are taking thoughts captive. Thoughts are internal, not external. The context does not include a principality. I think we errantly connect Ephesians 6 and Paul's discussion of principalities, powers, rulers of darkness, and spiritual wickedness in high places with this passage in 2 Corinthians. They are not connected and have different contexts.

A stronghold is a system of thought empowered by emotion. Have you ever tried to change an emotional person's mind? If you have, you know it is nearly impossible. Why? Because they are emotionally charged and connected to the belief system you are shining the light of God's Word on. You are addressing a stronghold in that person's life and they are protecting that stronghold with everything in them. When God's Word enters the heart of a person, it illuminates the strongholds, the arguments, and the high things that rise to exalt themselves against the knowledge of God.

9 : OVERCOMING TO REIGN

When God told Jeremiah he was ordained to be a prophet to the nations, the Word of God entered his heart and illuminated his thoughts. The corresponding thought in Jeremiah's heart rose up as a high thing to exalt itself against the knowledge of God. When Jeremiah embraced what God said, rather than the argument his heart presented, he won the thought-based spiritual warfare that was taking place in his own life. Jeremiah won a personal victory when he made his thought a prisoner of God's thought. That personal victory meant that he could now be effective as a prophet to the nations and deal with Kingdom issues beyond the scope of his personal life. Jeremiah took his own thoughts captive as an act of self-governance; self-governance leads to Kingdom governance beyond self. Jeremiah overcame to reign in the area of his purpose. Likewise, we must overcome to reign in the area of our purpose.

At this point, we could stop and say, "Wow, now I know the process God uses to help me eliminate unrighteous thoughts and ways that are not consistent with His thoughts and ways in heaven. God reveals a mystery to me, that revealed mystery highlights my wrong thoughts, I forsake those thoughts and ways and take them captive through an act of self-governance. I believe the thoughts God gave me and I have overcome. End of story." Yes and amen! Well, not so fast. The process is correct, but the ease with which we eliminate those thoughts and feelings depends on how deeply rooted the stronghold is in our hearts and/or our genetics. Yes, you read that correctly; how deeply rooted the stronghold is in our genetics. Now, let's talk about the iniquitous history recorded in our flesh.

At the beginning of this chapter, we said: "*To overcome is to reject the iniquitous genetic history and record passed down from our parents in favor of God's incorruptible seed that is the Word of God – just like Jesus overcame by rejecting the fallen genetics from Mary. It means that we reject the old and all that is from our former fallen nature and self-image to embrace what God has done for us and who He is in us, so we can reveal His image, thoughts, and ways to the creation.*"

Complete redemption means we are completely redeemed. If we are not walking in that redemption, it means we are living out of the residue of our former selves and the body of sin, not out of who we are as the body of Christ. We are still operating out of the memory of the law of sin and death in our fallen genome and conscious awareness rather than the law of the Spirit of life in Christ, with the mind of Christ. That is why we think, believe, and act a certain way at times and we do not understand why. That is what we will discuss next.

As a part of the redemptive process, it is important to understand the difference between sin and iniquity, which I believe are two different things. I define sin as an internal thought and/or outward act that misses the righteous mark (Matthew 5:28). Iniquity is more deeply rooted. It is the recorded law of sin and death in our flesh. Paul said it this way in Romans 7:25, "So then, with the mind, I myself serve the law of God, but with the flesh the law of sin." Paul said we serve the law of sin with our flesh. Jesus died so that we could be redeemed from the law of sin and death recorded in our fallen genetic construct, recorded in our flesh.

> Your body is a recorder; it records everything you have ever experienced.

Many years ago, I asked the Lord why I still had to deal with some of the same issues in life that I dealt with before I was born again. I said, "I didn't ask to be *born*, but I did ask to be *born-again*." So again, the question was, "Why?" He answered me immediately and said, "Because your body is a recorder, it records everything you have ever experienced." This becomes apparent for all of us when we get into a familiar environment; familiar environments often trigger or hit the play button on our body's recorded memories recreating the same feelings we had when we saw or experienced the original event. Often, the recreated feelings and emotions are so strong they can cause us to repeat the event or commit the same sin again. I've found this to be true based on personal experience.

I was in South Korea in 1983 and 1984. While there, I tasted and really liked a Korean dish called Yaki-mon-du. Yaki-mon-du is like pot stickers or oriental dumplings. On crisp, clear, cold nights, I would go into the village just outside the gate of the military base. The same vendor was there every night. I would hand him one United States Dollar and he would give me a bag of fresh, hot, deep-fried, Yaki-mon-du. I did this for much of the time I was there. Years later after returning home, if I walked outside on a crisp, clear, cold night, I would suddenly taste Yaki-mon-du. The environment literally triggered cellular memory that reproduced the taste in my mouth.

What did I do then? Since I could not find a Korean restaurant in my area, I experimented until I figured out how to make it myself. In other words, the physical manifestation of

9 : OVERCOMING TO REIGN

the memory was so strong and real that it drove me to learn how to make Yaki-mon-du so I could eat it anytime I wanted to. I literally could not handle the constant taste without experiencing Yaki-mon-du again. The tangible living memory drove me to engage in a past behavior until my body was satisfied.

I believe the manifestation of cellular memory brought about by the familiar environment of those crisp, clear, cold nights, demonstrates the principle of iniquitous behaviors and memories stored in our flesh. The iniquitous history can be activated by internal or external stimulus and cause physically recorded emotions and desires to be reintroduced and experienced in the present. It is the same as if we are engaged in the activity again, even though we are not. The regenerated strength of those emotions and desires are a stronghold that can lead us to re-engage in a previous activity. *A sin committed in, or observed by the flesh, will have a fleshly record of that sin. Unless it is dealt with, it is only a matter of time until something triggers it and we face it again.*

Here is another example. If I was standing in front of you and you saw and heard me clap three times in rapid succession, the memory would be recorded in the cells of your body for later recall. If I asked you a few moments later, you would say I clapped three times. Even though I did not touch you and you did not clap yourself, you would remember the event. What you experience in life is recorded in your body for recall, even if you are not the one who committed the act or the sin. What we see and hear can affect us just as strongly as what we have done ourselves, depending on how often we see and hear it, or how traumatic the event we witnessed or experienced was.

The brain does not retain every piece of information it receives or processes; however, the stronger and more frequent an experience, the greater the potential for retained cellular memory. In other words, a lifetime of activity is more deeply rooted, accessible, and retrievable than infrequent acts; unless of course, a single act was a traumatic event.

Today's technologies and scientific breakthroughs have given us insight into this reality. In the late 1990's, I read a book called, "*The Heart's Code*" by Paul Pearsall, Ph.D. The book gave numerous accounts of human organ transplant cases. In the cases highlighted in the book, after organ transplant recipients received an organ from a donor, they took on some of the *memories* and *lifestyle patterns* of the donor. The new behaviors were strikingly different from their own lifestyle patterns prior to receiving the donated organ.

Scientists say that cells share knowledge. The cells in the donated organ had stored lifestyle information and memories from the donor. Following the organ transplant, the stored lifestyle information from the donor was passed to the recipient's body through cellular interaction. In each of the cases cited by Dr. Pearsall, the receiving body conformed in some measure to the lifestyle behavior of the donor — even though the recipient had never met the donor. The recipients even experienced flashes of memory from the donor's life. I believe this speaks of cellular memory and gives clear insight into Proverbs 23:7, "As he thinks in his heart, so is he."

There is a stored physical and biological reality to life, to sin, and to iniquity (Romans 6:13,19). I personally refer to this as *"iniquitous toxicity."* Paul said it clearly for us in Romans 7, "But I see another law in my members, warring against the law of my mind, and bringing me into captivity to the law of sin, which is in my members" (Romans 7:23). I believe that is why God wants to regenerate our flesh towards the greater works. Regenerated flesh in partnership with the mind of Christ and the law of the Spirit of life in Christ does not contain a genetic or iniquitous record of our life and experiences. Past experiences have the potential to guide us away from God and His ways. It is also important to note that Paul asked the question, "O wretched man that I am! Who will deliver me from this body of death? I thank God through Jesus Christ our Lord" (Romans 7:24-25). Paul said that Jesus did!

There is a relatively new field of study in science called "epigenetics." Simply stated, epigenetics says memories and behavioral patterns of past generations can be stored genetically and passed to subsequent generations. In the case of epigenetics, it is passed on genetically through procreation rather than organ transplant. If this is truly the case, then not only do we receive genetic information that determines our physical attributes, but we can also receive genetically recorded behavioral, and/or, iniquitous attributes as well. That may be why we have a predisposed weakness in some areas, but not in others.

Laura and I have German Shepherds. We love the breed because of their intelligence and temperament; their temperament is how they behave because of breeding and genetics. We decided to breed our male and female, Rico and Jade. Jade gave birth to ten puppies and we kept one of the puppies for ourselves and named him Aslan.

German Shepherds are not an indigenous breed; the breed is just under 120 years old. Max von Stephanitz is credited with establishing the breed. He bred and inner-bred in the early 1900's to establish a breed of dog that would exhibit the traits he valued in a working dog.[6] I believe that presents itself as evidence of the epigenetic process. If animals do not possess the cognitive abilities of humanity, how is it they continue the behavioral patterns common to their breed? I believe genetic transference is the reason behind this phenomenon. I believe behavior patterns and generational memories can be encoded into DNA to be passed on to subsequent generations.

Just like various genes that determine our physical attributes can be dormant or dominant from generation to generation, I believe genetically recorded iniquitous patterns can be dormant or dominant as well. If a sin is repeated enough to become a lifestyle, I believe it *may* become an iniquitous pattern written and retained in our genetic code to be passed onto subsequent generations. I find it interesting that several places in scripture address the sins of the current generation, but the iniquities of their forefathers (Nehemiah 9:2; Jeremiah 11:10; and Daniel 9:16). I believe that to be, at least in some measure, a reference to generational iniquities passed on with a potential to become sin in the next generation.

I believe fasting proves this to be true as well. Isaiah said that one reason for fasting is that you "not hide yourself from your own flesh" (Isaiah 58:7). While there may be a variety of interpretations of what it means to "not hide yourself from your own flesh", I can tell you from personal experience one aspect of what it means.

Let's begin with what happens physically when you fast. You detoxify the cells in your body. If you have never fasted or have not fasted for a long time, it is likely you will experience the symptoms of a past cold or flu during, or shortly after the fast. Why? Because the toxins from a previous bout with a cold or the flu are stored in the cells of your body. When you fast, the body draws on the stored fat for nutrition and reintroduces the toxins into the bloodstream and you experience the symptoms again. I have experienced this myself.

---

6   http://gsrelite.co.uk/the-history-origin-of-the-german-shepherd-dog/

Not only have I experienced the physical symptoms of past sicknesses, but I have also experienced a flood of overwhelming and unwelcomed emotions. Physical toxins are stored in the body and so are "iniquitous toxins" that are the stored emotions of sin in the form of cellular memory. At different times when fasting, I would suddenly experience thoughts and feelings that I had not thought or felt for years. It was as if the memory in the cell was activated and released when my body drew on that cell for nutrition during the fast. I can truly say that I was not hiding from my flesh. My flesh was activated and repressed, rejected, and forgotten thoughts and feelings were made available for me to deal with before God in the fast.

I was a forgiven and godly man and had not engaged in the sinful thoughts or behaviors for many years, or in fact, had never engaged in some of the temptations that were present through very strong emotions and desires. Those memories surfaced as either cellular memory from my own life or *perhaps* genetic iniquities from a past generation. These things occurred during a fast so I could deal with that iniquitous history in Christ. Fasting is another form of conversing with God; your flesh initiates the conversation and God walks you out of your history and into your future.

I believe I was eliminating the "iniquitous toxicity" recorded and stored in the cells and genetic architecture of my body. I did not go on a search and destroy mission to find things about past generations and their sins, I was only dealing with the things that presented themselves during my fast. I was not addressing or focusing on the sins of my forefathers or their DNA, I was addressing my own body, my own genetic architecture. I was clearly not hiding from my flesh in the fast that God had chosen; my flesh was speaking loudly while staring me in the face (See Isaiah 58). *It is another example of blood having a voice. I believe sin and iniquity can take up physical residence in this fearfully and wonderfully made body of ours.* Whether it is there as a matter of our own personal sin experiences, through our observations of others, or an inherited genetic record. *I am not talking about past lives*; I am talking about cellular memory and a genetic record passed down through genetic transference.

This understanding may bring us to the point of wondering, "With all these things working against me, how am I ever to overcome my own thoughts and ways, and my inherited thoughts and ways?" This chapter is not so much about *what* we need to

9 : OVERCOMING TO REIGN

overcome as it is about *how* we overcome one step at a time. We overcome through conversations with God. God then helps us walk out of who we *were as the body of sin*, into who we *are as the resurrected body of Christ*. I am not fixing my genetic inheritance from past generations, I am replacing them by embracing my genetic inheritance in the blood of Christ.

God is redeeming every part of our existence. He did away with the body of sin and the genetic/epigenetic record of sin and death it contained. He gave us His Word, His Spirit, the law of the Spirit of life in Christ as the body of Christ, and the new covenant in His blood as a genetic contract. It is a contract to ensure our full redemption. The blood of Christ contains a genetic transference of the record of Christ to form Christ in us. A fallen nature, a fallen genome, unrighteous thoughts, and wicked ways were all addressed and dealt with on the cross of Christ where He died; where we died with Him. We left our old man behind when we were crucified, buried, and resurrected with Christ. All that is left are the genetic memories and residue of our former selves.

Overcoming to reign is the process God uses to walk us into the fullness of redemption. It is the process God uses to prepare us to govern with Him, to govern here on earth, and to govern in the ever-increasing expanse of His creation. When we overcome the residue of our former selves, we are preparing to reign beyond the limitation of self. Proper self-governance leads to kingdom governance beyond self. Our journey is more about what God has planned for us eternally than it is about our existence in a fallen creation; it is about our eternal purpose. God has drawn us into the Godhead to operate out of who He is. *In that day, you will know that I am in the Father, you in Me and I in you.* Today is that day; seize the day through the process of overcoming to reign in cooperation with communion, the Word of God, and the law of the Spirit of life in Christ that abides in us as the body of Christ.

CHAPTER 10: REDEMPTION – THE BIG PICTURE

At this point, I think it is important to combine what we have learned in Chapters 1 – 9. It will help create a big picture before we move on. This chapter is designed to be a bridge between what we have learned and what we are about to learn. I will add a few new and clarifying thoughts as well.

Many times, we make the mistake of taking a piece of a puzzle and acting as if it is the whole. We often do that with things like stand-alone faith or stand-alone grace. Each piece is important, but while each has a measure of stand-alone truth, they create a much fuller and richer picture of redemption together than they do as separate individual pieces. I've decided to use this chapter to serve as a synergistic partial summary that ensures understanding before moving through the rest of the chapters. I do not want to leave anything open to misinterpretation. I truly want you to know what I am saying so you can either receive or reject the premise of this book on your own – based on your own judgment and relationship with the Lord.

I am not trying to convince anyone to believe what I am presenting; that is not my job. I am simply sharing biblical truths that have the potential to transform the life of a reader if mixed with faith. The choice to agree or disagree based on your doctrinal view is completely up to you. As you read or learn new things from this book, rather than outright rejecting things that are new to you, engage the process of overcoming to reign as a part of your transformational process.

The primary focus of this book is that God is merging five areas: God and man, the heavens and the earth, time and eternity, the government of heaven and the governments of earth, and the communities of heaven and the communities of earth.

When God descended to become Jesus of Nazareth, God enacted the first merger: God and man, God as a man. The merger of God and man facilitated the restoration of humanity, which includes the human genome, and a resulting merger of the remaining four areas through restored humanity. By merging with man, God has made restored humanity the focal point and primary mechanism in creation for the coming of His will and His Kingdom on earth as it is in heaven.

This is where I am going to introduce a new thought and clarified position I purposely have not addressed prior to this point. The first Adam was a living soul, and Jesus, the Last Adam, was a life-giving spirit. Here it is: *those are two completely different levels of being.* Jesus, the life-giving spirit, reversed every action of the soul being, the first Adam. As a life-giving spirit, He placed the form of God in the form of man. We are now spirit born from above. That is why we are a new creature; something that never existed before. Not only did Jesus reverse the actions of the first Adam, He gave us all spiritual life.

The first Adam was created in the image of God with the ability to bear His likeness through ongoing relationship but he was not a spirit being. He was a living soul with living DNA that was encoded with the image of God, with the capacity to take on the ever-increasing likeness of God. His body and soul were united so the soul had the ability to interact with the body and the body with the soul to reveal the image and ever-increasing likeness of God. When Adam ate of the tree, he activated the law of sin and death. The law of sin and death replaced the image and likeness of God through degraded DNA. The law of sin and death took up residence within the genome of humanity and was passed from generation to generation through the God-ordained procreative process He established and blessed in Genesis. Remember, everyone who would ever live would come from that genome.

When Adam ate of the tree, his DNA was rewritten to be an expression of the law of sin and death. The soul also took on the nature of sin and death. The body and the soul were united to express the new sin and death-based genetic architecture. Sin was embedded in the genome of mankind. The consciousness of mankind partnered with that genetic programming to make mankind the expression of sin and death contained within that genome. The result is sin and death. The human body was now the body of sin. Sin took dominion over man to exercise dominion over the creation through man.

The next thing we see is that Cain slew Abel. As we said in Chapter 4, the blood-based sacrifice of Abel opened a door, a gateway, that granted wholesale entrance to sin and to the kingdom of darkness. All world systems have operated from that foundation ever since.

When Jesus the Last Adam became flesh, it was to redeem flesh. When Jesus brought the Kingdom of God, it was to replace and override the kingdoms of this world that gained entrance through Cain. Just like all humanity that would ever exist was in the first Adam, we were also in the genome of Christ when He was born, baptized, crucified, and resurrected. But beyond the reversal of the actions of Adam and Cain, Jesus came as a life-giving spirit to introduce the form of God into the form of man. *The form of God was in Christ; it was not in the first Adam — God did not live in the first Adam.*

As a life-giving spirit, Jesus did away with the body of sin and gave believing humanity an upgrade. He took us beyond the Adamic partnership of living soul and genetics, designed to express the image and likeness of God in the creation, and made us new creation beings born from above. That is evidenced in John 20:22, "And He breathed on them and said receive the Holy Spirit." That was the "born from above" experience for the disciples. Jesus, the life-giving spirit, breathed on the disciples the same way God breathed the breath of life into the nostrils of the first Adam when He became a living soul. As we said in a previous chapter, humanity can now receive God in an earthen vessel the same way Jesus filled the emptied form of man with the emptied form of God. When God created Adam, he was a living soul. Through Jesus the life-giving spirit, we are new creatures: The Spirit form of God in man. That is our upgraded and elevated condition.

As we said previously, the first Adam was a type of the Last Adam. Let's explain the typology a bit further. At first, we limited the type-for-type explanation to the parallel actions of the two Adams. But now, we will carry that further. The reason the first Adam was a type, is because He did not carry the fullness of God the way Jesus did. The first Adam was a living soul with living DNA, a prototype of Him who was to come. He was created as a pure soul with pure genetics. The Last Adam contained the fullness of the Godhead and as a life-giving spirit, He gave us the same ability. There is now no greater potential or higher form of humanity. As we said in Chapter 8, that is the greater works. It is the full expression of God in and through man. God can be seen through our new creation spirit, soul, and body, including restored genetics through the blood of Jesus because we are the body of Christ.

Before the cross, God anointed flesh because He could not take up residence within the form of man. God anoints the sons of men. That is why Jesus was anointed as the Son of Man. The church has primarily focused on developing the gifts of the Spirit as the pinnacle of redemption until the return of Christ, but that is the lesser work. Our ability, through Christ, to fully express God is the greater work. Now, through the process of faith and overcoming to reign, we are transformed into the full image of God so we can release His Kingdom and give the creation something to respond to.

We have been born from above to fully express God in the creation. We are more than the first Adam ever was; he had life, but we have life more abundantly because we are spirit, not merely a soul. We have been fully realigned to be a descendant of the Adam who never fell. We are called to see and release the Kingdom that has yet to come in the measure God desires.

If we do not understand the fullness of redemption, we will continue to live a life well below the life Jesus died to give us. The very life most of us are already dissatisfied with is a life out of the soul, living the genetically recorded and repeated patterns of our past. If we are really blessed, we are walking in some measure of the lesser works which makes us feel better about ourselves — like we are doing something for God. But we must not stop at feeling better about ourselves because the gifts God graced us with are operating in our lives. We must keep moving forward to the high calling of God in Christ. We must know we are new creatures called to release the Kingdom of God in the earth. We will find out how as we talk about the heavens and the earth, time and eternity, and the Kingdom of God in the next several chapters.

10 : REDEMPTION – THE BIG PICTURE

CHAPTER 11: THE HEAVENS AND THE EARTH

In the beginning, God created the heavens and the earth. As I am sure you already know, that is the first verse in the Bible, Genesis 1:1. The first thing God mentions in the whole of scripture, in the very same sentence, is the creation of the heavens and the earth. Why? Because it is the context for the rest of scripture *and* it is the environmental context for His relationship with mankind. Everything from that point forward is within the context of the heavens, the earth, and the beings within them. Whether God Himself, mankind, the cloud of witnesses or heavenly beings, the environmental context from Genesis to Revelation is the heavens and the earth.

God created the heavens and the earth with the intent that the two should be one in expression the same way He wants unity with, and between, God and man. In John 17:21, Jesus prayed, "that they all may be one, as You, Father, are in Me, and I in You; that they also may be one in Us." That is unity between God and man and man's invitation into the Godhead in Christ. In the Lord's Prayer, Jesus said to pray that our Father's Kingdom and His will would be on *earth* as it is in *heaven* (Matthew 6:10). That is unity between heaven and earth through the unity of God and man.

God never intended for the environments or substances of heaven and earth to be separated. Just like the relationship between God and man, the relationship between the heavens and the earth was severed by the fall. As such, redemption includes the merger of God and man, *and* the heavens and the earth. God did not create the heavens and the earth so the man He created in His image would be restricted to the earth alone. Even if Adam did not have the ability to move beyond the earth in his early state of maturity, I believe it was to be a part of his matured future.

If we truly believe God created the heavens, the earth, and mankind, we must start thinking as a people who know our limitless God made us in His image and ever-increasing likeness. If our God and Father did not intend for us to operate in the heavens with Him, then why did He raise us up to be seated there in Christ the moment we received Him? When we accepted Christ, we were born *from above* and God immediately expanded the environment of our relationship with Him beyond the earth into the heavens. He merged the separated environments of heaven and earth in Christ, and subsequently, in believing humanity.

> ...and raised us up together, and made us sit together in the heavenly places in Christ Jesus. Ephesians 2:6

> Blessed be the God and Father of our Lord Jesus Christ, who has blessed us with every spiritual blessing in the heavenly places in Christ.
> Ephesians 1:3

Not only did God raise us up to be seated in heavenly places, He also blessed us with every spiritual blessing in heavenly places. He started by blessing the man and the woman. Now, He has restored that blessing to us in the heavens and the earth, in Christ, the Word made flesh now glorified (Genesis 1:28). If we are not able to access the heavens, if we do not abide in the heavens with literal access to them, then we have no access to the spiritual blessings God says He blessed us with.

An earthbound worldview has become our own self-imposed limitation. It is not a limitation placed on us by God who raised us up into the heavens. We have been raised with Christ. Our entire paradigm in the Western first-world church is earth-based with an earthbound, non-heavenly perspective. Other cultures around the world clearly have a greater understanding of humanity's innate spirituality. The Western church along with its intellectual foundation has limited our spiritual insight and understanding to earthly paradigms. We were born and raised in the prison of a fallen reality apart from God with no understanding or conscious awareness of the heavens. Our natural perceptive ability includes only an awareness of our physical earthly surroundings. That is why Paul told us to set our minds on things above.

> If then you were raised with Christ, seek those things which are above, where Christ is, sitting at the right hand of God. Set your mind on things above, not on things on the earth.
> For you died and your life is hidden with Christ in God.
> Colossians 3:1-3

Our fallen senses are connected to a fallen world and therefore create a fallen worldview. Those worldviews form a belief system and way of life that operates according to developed earthly systems that are contrary to the Kingdom and will of God. They are the philosophies, empty deceit, traditions of men, and the basic principles of the world. When we think like the world systems we were born into, we become one with them and perpetuate them through our mental and physical participation with their "shadow of death" systemic processes.

> God does not want us to redecorate the wilderness and then call it the Promised Land. He does not want it on earth as it is already somewhere on earth, He wants it on earth as it is in heaven.

If we set our minds on earthly things, if we get our vision from the earth, *it will only be on earth as it already is on earth.* We will simply repeat and strengthen what we see here. Because humanity was created in the image and likeness of God, our Creator, we will always endeavor to create within the created realm. It is inherent to human nature, even the fallen human nature. We will endeavor to improve our surroundings and to redecorate the wilderness with our God-given creativity. God does not want us to redecorate the wilderness and then call it the Promised Land. God does not want it on earth as it is already somewhere on earth; He is not interested in perpetuating earthly systems. He sent Jesus to be the door between the heavens and the earth — *so it can be on earth as it is in heaven* — when we abide in Him and He abides in us (Matthew 6:10, John 10:7).

When we think like the heavens *we have been raised to in Christ*, we perpetuate on earth what we have seen in heaven. We are born from above and abide in heaven with the ability to see there. Jesus said, "Except a man be born from above he cannot see the Kingdom of Heaven" (John 3:3). That means if we *are* born from above, *we can see the Kingdom of Heaven*. Jesus saw what His Father in heaven was doing and then did that on earth, all so it would be on earth as it is in heaven (John 5:19).

When we talked about Jesus and the lesser works we found this truth. "*No one has ascended to heaven but He who came down from heaven, that is, the Son of Man who is in heaven*" (John 3:13; emphasis added). Jesus was in the form of God and equal with God. When Jesus left heaven, He descended into the earth as the Son of God to become the Son of Man. Jesus made it very clear that He came down from heaven, but not only that, *He also ascended back to heaven*. He *descended* as the Son of God and *ascended* as the Son of Man.

He made it clear that He was in heaven while He was speaking to them, "*the Son of Man who is in heaven*." Jesus said He was in heaven while He was standing on the earth. That means He was in both places at once and living according to the full landscape and environment God created for His relationship with man: the heavens and the earth. Jesus was a walking, talking, living, breathing expression of the merger of God and man, and heaven and earth in a human body. That is how God created us to operate, as the central focus of creation, operating in both realms while bearing and revealing the image and likeness of God Himself. It cannot be on earth as it is in heaven if we cannot see heaven. God has given new creation mankind access to both realms so that through man, the earth would be united with heaven and the ways of God in heaven.

> Let us make man in our image and according to our likeness.
> Genesis 1:26

> And the Lord God formed man from the dust of the ground, and breathed into his nostrils the breath of life; and man became a living being.
> Genesis 2:7

When God made man, man was created in His image and according to His likeness.

11: THE HEAVENS AND THE EARTH

Man bore, in some measure, the image of the Creator. When God formed man, He formed him from the dust of the creation; man bore the image of the creation. Since man bore the image of both the Creator and the creation, He had access to God and the fullness of the creation.

When God created Adam, he was a son of God (Luke 3:38). According to Job 1:6, sons of God have access to the heavens and to the Lord. "Now there was a day when the sons of God came to present themselves before the Lord." When Adam fell, he lost his place of sonship and the image of God he was created in; but he retained the image of the creation. Adam was then relegated to the earthly creation whose image he bore.

Why could Jesus ascend back to the heavens? Because He was God's Son. The heavens recognized the DNA in His blood and He bore the image and likeness of God. That very image gave Him access to the full environment God created for His relationship with mankind; He had access to both the heavens and the earth. As we have said repeatedly, Jesus was the reintroduction of the image and likeness of God in the earth. The reintroduction of the image and likeness of God in the earth reopened the heavens to mankind.

> When He had been baptized, Jesus came up immediately from the water; and behold, *the heavens were opened to Him*, and He saw the Spirit of God descending like a dove and alighting upon Him. And suddenly *a voice came from heaven*, saying, "This is my beloved *Son*, in whom I am well pleased."
> Matthew 3:16-17 (emphasis added)

Matthew said the heavens were opened to Him. That means prior to that moment, the heavens were not opened to Him. The heavens opened to God's Son at His baptism and they are now open to redeemed and restored sons of God. Adam heard the voice of God in the garden when he fell and Jesus heard the voice of God through an open heaven at His baptism. Jesus is "the way" back into the heavens and our relationship with God. He is the only way. Why do they need to be open for us? So we can enter the fullness of the relationship Jesus died to give us. So we can get our vision from heaven and not from the earth, and so humanity can step into the fullness of our destiny as sons of God.

This is clearly evidenced by Jacob's ladder in Genesis 28:12-13, and the words of Jesus in John 1:51.

> Then he dreamed, and behold, a ladder was set up on the earth, and its top reached to heaven, and there the angels of God were ascending and descending on it. And behold, the Lord stood above it and said: "I am the Lord God of Abraham your father and the God of Isaac; the land on which you lie I will give to you and your descendants."
> Genesis 28:12-13

> Most assuredly, I say to you, hereafter you shall see heaven open, and the angels of God ascending and descending upon the Son of Man.
> John 1:51

In both cases, angels were ascending and descending between heaven and earth. In Jacob's dream, it records the Lord was on top of the ladder, and in John, the Lord Jesus was on the earth. Jesus was fully engaged with heaven and the angelic realm. The passage in John reveals the open pathway between the heavens and the earth to facilitate the merger of the five areas we spoke of in Chapter 1: God and man, heaven and earth, time and eternity, the government of heaven and the governments of earth, and the communities of heaven and the communities of earth.

God has unified God and man, and heaven and earth, in and through Jesus. We must have this understanding to walk in the fullness of restoration and to bring heaven to earth as God desires. This is where the church is missing it today and we are in trouble. How are we in trouble? We are in trouble because we get our vision from the earth. We get our vision from an earthly worldview, from our political leanings, and from the understanding of life we have gained from our existence in a fallen creation subject to the basic principles of the world. As a result, we make our decisions from that worldview. Do we ask God about which politician to vote for, or do we gravitate towards the lesser of two evils or the one who *seems* to most closely reflect our values?

The government of heaven cannot merge with the governments of earth if we focus only on earthly governments apart from the Kingdom of God and His will. We must receive our vision from heaven, not from worldviews based on earthly experiences or the traditions of men. We have access to the heavens in Christ to give Christ access to people, cultures, and governments in the earth through us.

11: THE HEAVENS AND THE EARTH

While Christ is the door to the sheep, we are the gates in the earth through which the Kingdom and will of God pass into this realm. The Psalmist said,

> Lift up your heads, O you gates!
> And be lifted up you everlasting doors! And the King of glory shall come in.
> Psalm 24:7

We are those gates; we are those *lifted-up* everlasting doors. We cannot neglect our role in the coming of God's Kingdom and will into the earth. The present kingdoms of this world were not formed by pre-fall Adam in partnership with God. They were formed after the fall and after systemic sin entered through the door opened through Cain. As a result, they do not look like heaven or God's plan for the earth. That is why Jesus told us to pray that our Father's Kingdom would come and His will would be done on earth as it is in heaven. It is not yet "on earth as it is in heaven" and it will not be if we continue to get our vision from the earth.

> *And He showed me a pure river of water of life,*
> *clear as crystal, proceeding from the throne of God and of the Lamb.*
> Revelation 22:1

To further clarify, the "on earth as it is in heaven" pattern is clearly evidenced in heaven, creation, and in believing Spirit-filled humanity. In heaven, there is the throne of God and of the Lamb and a river flowing from their midst. Have you ever wondered why there are three members of the Godhead, Father, Son, and Holy Spirit, but only the throne of God and the Lamb? It is because *Holy Spirit is the river* that proceeds from the throne and carries the substance of everything that flows from God and the Lamb. So, what do we have here? We have two persons of the Godhead with a river flowing from their midst in heaven.

How interesting it is to note that God created two people in His image and put them in a garden with a river flowing from their midst (Genesis 2:10). Why? Because He wants it on earth as it is in heaven; it has been His intent from the beginning. *God used heaven as the template for the earth and Himself as the template for mankind.* Both having the ultimate purpose of one looking like and expressing the other. We can carry this further by looking at the same pattern in believers.

Jesus said that Holy Spirit would live within us. He also said that He and His Father would make their home in us (John 14:17, 23). In John 7:38-39, Jesus said rivers of living water would flow out of our hearts, speaking of Holy Spirit as the river who lives in us. Interesting, two persons of the Godhead in heaven with a river flowing from their midst; two people made in the image of God on earth with a river flowing from their midst, and believers with God the Father and God the Son living in us with Holy Spirit as rivers of living water flowing from our midst. Does any of this sound familiar? It is the same exact pattern in heaven, on earth, and in believers. That is why He told us to pray that His Father's Kingdom would come and His will would be done on earth as it is in heaven. God clearly wants it on earth as it is in heaven.

Here are a few things to note about what Jesus told us to pray: 1. The Father is in heaven and His Kingdom and His will are in operation there, 2. Jesus would not tell us to pray for the Father's Kingdom to come and His will to be done on earth as they are in heaven if they were already in operation on earth the way they are in heaven, 3. Jesus would not tell us to pray for the Father's Kingdom to come and His will to be done on earth as it is in heaven unless the Father wanted it on earth the way it is in heaven, 4. Jesus would not tell us to pray for something that His Father did not intend on answering to the fullest — through those praying for the coming of His Kingdom and will on earth as it is in heaven.

God's heart has always been for it to be on earth as it is in heaven. That is why He created the heavens and the earth, and that is why He created and redeemed mankind. He is uniting heaven and earth today by revealing and releasing the fullness of Christ, His heavenly Kingdom, and His heavenly will through His relationship with us. *It can only be on earth as it is in heaven when the Kingdom of God is released through those of us who live in heaven, see in heaven, speak in heaven and live on earth. It is released through those of us who live in both places.* The part of the Kingdom God shows us is the part of the Kingdom He wants to reveal through us; that is our assignment. We are the gates and the everlasting doors the King of Glory passes through to fill the earth with Himself and His ways; and we are the gates and the everlasting doors through which eternity passes to manifest in time.

11: THE HEAVENS AND THE EARTH

CHAPTER 12: TIME AND ETERNITY

Time and eternity are different dimensions; you can draw on one to affect the other. They are separate but connected. Things can be finished in eternity, but not yet manifest in time. Because we are born *within time*, we have a chronological *time-based* paradigm and often have difficulty seeing beyond it. God placed *eternity* in the hearts of men and we are connected to both *time* and *eternity; time and eternity merge in us* (Ecclesiastes 3:11).

Time can be viewed as the incremental passing of measurable moments within this dimension. This is defined by the Greek word *chronos*. Chronos is the Greek root for the English word "chronology." Another biblical definition of time is defined by the Greek word *kairos*. This word is used when speaking of an appointed time in the purpose of God. We will not be dealing with specific definitions of time in this chapter, we will speak of time in the general context as compared to eternity. With one exception, we will discuss *the fullness of time* and its meaning in the book of Galatians.

Unlike time, eternity has no time-based reference and is considered infinite and unending. From a theological perspective, eternity does not have a beginning or an end but is something that has always existed and will always exist, just like God who is eternal.

History is full of recorded events and measurable moments within the creation that God released into time from His eternal realm. Since eternity exists outside the dimension of time and is not bound by it, eternity supersedes time. God created time, therefore time is subordinate to God. When God created humanity in His image, He gave them a connection to both time and eternity. Humanity and their faith in God are the central mechanisms through which eternal truths and realities are released into time and the created realm we have been given dominion over.

> Time and eternity and heaven and earth merge in us
> through faith in God, and faith in His Word.

In God's eternal paradigm, He views prophesied, appointed, and preordained events as *finished in eternity.* In fact, prophetic words are sourced in the already completed work revealed by the prophetic word. While they are finished in eternity, they have a planned passage from the eternal timeless realm into the time-based, created realm under heaven. The interesting thing is, anyone who did anything significant for God did not live according to the *chronos* generational dispensation of their natural lives — they lived based on a vision and revelation of eternal truths connected to a future day. The day they saw was finished in eternity, but not yet manifest on the timeline of human history. They believed and brought the new thing they saw, the coming day of the Lord, into their personal now.

We must understand that God does not wait on time to release the reality or fruit of an eternal truth when someone in the earth, within time, apprehends it by faith *ahead of the fullness of time appointed for the actual event.* When that happens, time and eternity have merged through faith in God and His Word.

As we said earlier, the only definition of time we will address is the fullness of time in Galatians. "When the fullness of time had come, God sent forth His Son born of a woman, born under the law" (Galatians 4:4). In this case, the word *chronos* is used to indicate that the chronological time for the incarnate appearance of God's Son had reached its full measure. In fact, the year of Christ's birth became the point of reference for chronological time. That is why we use B.C. and A.D. — before Christ (B.C.) and anno Domini (A.D.). Anno Domini literally means "in the year of our Lord." Christ's birth became the focal point of chronological *chronos* time. Even so, God has never required us to wait on the chronological manifestation of an event to engage the truth that event facilitates. In other words, God does not need to wait for the completion of a time-based earthly event to

12 : TIME AND ETERNITY

release the eternal truth and blessing it represents.

Eternal truth is not held prisoner by the associated physical event that is waiting to be expressed in the created realm. *We must be able to differentiate between a God-initiated event that lands on the timeline of human history and the pre-existent eternal reality that gave rise to that event.* What does that mean? It means we can access the eternal reality and benefits of an event before the event occurs within time. It is settled in heaven before it lands on earth. "Forever, oh Lord; Your word is settled in heaven" (Psalm 119:89). In the church world, we are familiar with two specific passages regarding time.

> *While the earth remains, seedtime and harvest, cold and heat,*
> *winter and summer, and day and night shall not cease.*
> Genesis 8:22 (emphasis added)

> *To everything there is a season,*
> *a time for every purpose under heaven.*
> Ecclesiastes 3:1 (emphasis added)

Genesis says that while the earth remains there will be seedtime and harvest. Seedtime and harvest is an earthly operation; there will be seedtime and harvest in the earth. Ecclesiastes says there is a *time* for every purpose *under heaven*. Both passages mention time. Though we may be familiar with these two passages, it is important to note the environmental context for their application — *the earth, under heaven*.

God made it very clear where time applies, *in the earth* and *under heaven*. What if I told you that you could eat the fruit of a tree that would not be planted for another 2000 years? You may say, "That is not possible." I beg to differ; there is scriptural evidence to the contrary.

When Jesus was speaking with the Jews in John 8, He said, "Your father Abraham rejoiced to see My day, he saw it and was glad." The problem is, Abraham lived 2000 chronological years before the fullness of time, before the day of Christ. Abraham saw Christ's day 2000 years in advance. What is even more incredible is that Abraham received bread and wine from Melchizedek. Abraham saw the day of Christ and received communion 2000 years before the cross. In other words, Abraham ate the pre-existent eternal fruit of the cross of

Christ 2000 years before the tree of Christ's suffering was planted.

Abraham did not have to wait on the chronological progression of time to receive the eternal truth and benefit of the cross. By faith, Abraham believed in the Lord and His work on the cross. As a result, God credited it to him as righteousness as if the crucifixion had already occurred within the chronology of time (Genesis 15:6). Abraham's faith brought the eternal truth and record of the cross into his personal life before the fullness of time. He believed the gospel and mixed it with faith 2000 years before the incarnation of Christ. Believed the gospel you say? Yes. The writer of Hebrews made that abundantly clear.

> Therefore, since a promise remains of entering His rest, let us fear lest any of you seem to have come short of it. For indeed the *gospel* was preached to us *as well as to them*; but the word which they heard did not profit them, *not being mixed with faith* in those who heard it. For we who have believed to enter that rest, as He has said: "So I swore in My wrath, 'They shall not enter My rest,'" *although the works were finished from the foundation of the world.*
> Hebrews 4:1–4 (emphasis added)

The writer of Hebrews said the *gospel* was preached to them and the works were finished from the foundation of the world. Why were the works finished from the foundations of the world? Because the Lamb of God was slain before the foundation of the world. The gospel and associated rest were available before the fullness of time, before the day and incarnation of Christ. In the heart and mind of God, His works were eternally finished and the gospel was made available by faith regardless of the dispensation of chronological time.

The children of Israel did not enter God's *available rest* because they did not mix faith with the available eternal truth God revealed to them, the truth of Christ's redemptive work on the cross. Abraham, the father of faith, saw the day of Christ and mixed it with faith to receive the fruit of the gospel in his life. What is rest? Rest is the faith-based assurance that we have access to all God has made available through the finished work of Christ, regardless of the dispensation of time we live in, or the current state of world affairs.

We can operate out of the eternal and available finished work of God, works that were finished from the foundation of the world right now. The works were finished before the world was created. Abraham understood that, but the children of Israel did not.

12 : TIME AND ETERNITY

Some might say that Abraham was special because he was the father of faith. Again, I beg to differ. There was another biblical figure that saw the same day Abraham saw. Psalm 118:24 records the same phrase that Jesus spoke of Abraham. This is the *day* the Lord has made, we will *rejoice* and be *glad* in it. How interesting. Jesus said, "Abraham *rejoiced* to see My *day*; he saw it and was *glad*." The psalmist saw the same day and said the same thing as Abraham. He saw and embraced the same day, but this time, 1000 chronological years before the fullness of time and the cross.

Whether you believe the "psalmist" is David or not, the pattern of not following the law and living out of a pre-existent eternal day is clearly a pattern that David followed. He ate the showbread, the bread of the presence, bread that was reserved for the priests alone. Jesus said He was the bread of life that came down from heaven (John 6:48-51). Jesus said, "Give us this day our daily bread." Jesus said, "This bread is My body given to you." Just like Abraham received communion with Melchizedek 2000 years before the cross, David ate the bread of life, the body of Jesus, 1000 years before the bread of life came down from heaven.

Furthermore, David built the tabernacle which housed the presence of God. David ate the bread of the presence and then hosted the Arc of the Covenant and the presence of God. Those who entered the tabernacle began to prophesy as if Holy Spirit had already been poured out on all flesh, and as if Joel Chapter 2 and Acts Chapter 2 had already occurred. David ate the body of Jesus, hosted the presence of God, and prophesied as if he had already received the gospel and the baptism of the Holy Spirit.

The reality is, the eternal truth unfettered by time in the realm of heaven and eternity, considered those future timeline events as complete. If it exists as an eternal truth in heaven, it is finished and accessible in the heart and mind of God. When God looked upon Abraham and David, He found two people of faith in the earth (*within time and under heaven*) who did not wait on time to live out of a pre-existent eternal truth, the day of Christ they saw and knew was coming.

If Abraham or David had waited on time to bring them what their faith in God and heaven made available to them, they would have died without experiencing the works that were finished from the foundation of the world. There would have been no Isaac, no Jacob, no Nation of Israel, and no king named David who experienced the presence of God in greater measure than most Christians do today. Abraham preceded the law and David lived in the time of the law, but neither lived according to the chronological dispensation of time they were physically born into. They lived by faith in God and the eternal day of redemption they saw coming. They saw that day and embraced it by faith. Because of their faith, God gave it to them without regard for the "fullness of time" chronological arrival of that day in the created realm, on earth, under heaven.

It seems that Abraham and David had a better understanding of living by faith than we do. They had a better understanding of the day they saw than we do. They rejoiced and were glad about the eternal day of salvation. Many today lament it and keep waiting for Jesus to rescue us from the world that needs the eternal truths we are supposed to embody and release into the creation as co-creators with God. We have a better covenant with better promises, yet they lived a fuller life and relationship with God than most of us do. Time, and the dispensation of time they lived in, did not dictate what Abraham or David received from God; their faith did. Time was not their master. If that is not enough, there is yet another example in Matthew 8:14-17, when Jesus healed Peter's mother-in-law.

> Now when Jesus had come into Peter's house, He saw his wife's mother lying sick with a fever. So, He touched her hand, and the fever left her. And she arose and served them. When evening had come, they brought to Him many who were demon-possessed. And He cast out the spirits with a word, and healed all who were sick, *that it might be fulfilled which was spoken by Isaiah the prophet, saying, "He Himself took our infirmities and bore our sicknesses."*
> (emphasis added)

How interesting. The scripture Matthew is referring to is Isaiah 53:4. Matthew 8:14-17 says Jesus cast out spirits with a word and healed all who were sick, "*that it might be fulfilled which was spoken by Isaiah the prophet, saying 'He Himself took our infirmities and bore our sicknesses.'*" There is only one problem with that. Jesus had not gone to the cross yet, so He had not taken our infirmities or bore our sicknesses while on earth, in time, under heaven. How was He operating out of the fulfillment of a prophetic scripture that had not been fulfilled or fallen on the timeline of human history yet?

It is very simple. Jesus was not restricted to chronological time-based events any more

12 : TIME AND ETERNITY

than Abraham, or David were. He was drawing on the pre-existent eternal truth of what His death, burial, and resurrection would bring even though they had not yet occurred as a manifest event on an earthly timeline under heaven. Jesus was healing and operating out of the eternal truth and finished work of the cross even though He had not yet gone to the cross. That is also how Jesus forgave sins before the cross and raised the dead before His resurrection — *the law of the Spirit of life in Christ has made me free from the law of sin and death.* Jesus operated out of the fulfillment of the law of the Spirit of life in Christ, even though He had not been crucified, buried, or resurrected.

> Jesus forgave sins before the cross and raised the dead before His resurrection because time was not His master.

You may be wondering what all this talk about time and eternity has to do with the life of the believer today. It is simple: this understanding removes the conflict and tension between what is coming in its manifest fullness as a corporate timeline event, and the fruit of that event already available in eternity to those who embrace it by faith. God, heaven, and eternity have made preexistent heaven-based eternal truths available now to faith-filled believers living on earth, in time, under heaven.

Today's question is, what has God and eternity made available that you are waiting on time to give you? Unfortunately, it seems the church grants more power to the dimension of time and the "church-age" than it does God and His Word.

As we said earlier, when we do not understand how or why God does something, we errantly place those events under the heading of the sovereignty of God. If we cannot explain how these things happened in the lives of Abraham, David, and Jesus, we say it was a sovereign move or act of God. We call it sovereignty if we cannot explain it, but then violate that very sovereignty by restricting God to the boundaries of the things we claim to understand. We cannot say God is sovereign and then oppose that very sovereignty by telling others what God will and will not do based on the dispensation of time we live in. Time is not a boundary or barrier to the release of eternal truths into the earth; our lack of vision and faith are the only things that stop the eternal from entering time through us. Believing humanity is the focal point and mechanism for the release of the eternal realities God has made available to us.

There is ample scripture to show we do not have to submit to time as if time is our God and master. Abraham and David believed God and He responded to them from eternity *according to their faith, not according to a dispensation of time*. We cannot use the idea of dispensations of time (the incremental passing of measurable moments within this dimension) as our foundational justification to reject the manifestation of eternal truths because they do not fit our doctrinal timeline or eschatological views.

Our whole emphasis is on a time-based eschatological view of the end of the world. But God is not interested in ending the world; He was crucified, buried, and resurrected to save it and its inhabitants.

God has made the full restoration of believing humanity available to us today. He made the body and blood of Jesus available to Abraham. He made the body of Christ available to David when he ate the showbread, and He made the outpouring of His Spirit available in David's tabernacle. God is no respecter of persons; He has made the eternal reality of what Jesus purchased for us available now. He made the eternal reality of the cross available before the cross was planted, and He has made the eternal reality of the resurrection and the full redemption of believing humanity available before His second coming and the restoration of all things. He has made the restoration of all things available before the corporate manifestation of the restoration of all things. *By faith, we use time to access eternity and God's forever settled in heaven eternal truths.*

We have made the mistake of thinking corporately rather than individually when it comes to the promises of God and their availability. We are errantly waiting for preordained prophetic events to land on the timeline of human history as the manifestation of all-encompassing eternal truths that will affect every believer, such as the rapture and long awaited twinkling of an eye transformation of believing humanity. *But, neither Abraham nor David waited for the corporate availability or manifestation of the day of Christ to access it personally.* So why should we wait on a corporate Kingdom event before we believe for and receive the fruit of that Kingdom event personally? We can believe and receive just like Abraham, David, and Jesus. *They used time to access eternity.*

The restoration of human genetics and a glorified body is something every believer is looking forward to. It is something Jesus secured for us as an eternal truth awaiting

12 : TIME AND ETERNITY

physical manifestation when He returns to administrate His Kingdom on earth, when we see Him as He is (1 John 3:2). So, the question is, do I have to wait for His corporate return to see Him as He is and to access the resurrection and regeneration of my body?

As I share an experience with you, please do not stop reading because you have a different eschatological view than I do. A year or so ago, I was having a specific conversation with the Lord. For two days, I had two rapture songs going through my head and I could not get rid of them. The moment I woke up, I heard the songs in my head. Finally, I asked the Lord this question, "Lord, why are you filling my head with these songs when you know I don't believe in the traditional version of the rapture anymore?" His immediate answer surprised me, He said, "Who said I said anything about a corporate event?" Suddenly, I understood. He was talking about an *individual rapturous encounter with Him* that could and would result in a transformation of my personal life. I can access the resurrection before the resurrection.

That may sound "out there" to some, but did it sound "out there" when Abraham believed in the Lord 2000 years before the cross (Genesis 15:6)? The same Abraham who was not weak in faith and did not consider *his own body, already dead* (Romans 4:19). Did it sound "out there" when Jesus said, "Whoever eats my flesh and drinks my blood has eternal life, and I will raise him up the last day?" I chose those scriptures on purpose. "Your father Abraham rejoiced to see My day, he saw it and was glad." And, "Abraham was not weak in faith and did not consider his own body, already dead." God gave Abraham the day he saw 2000 years early and it affected his body (Genesis 15:6; John 8:56; Romans 4:19). "Whoever eats my flesh and drinks my blood has eternal life, and I will raise him up the last day" (John 6:54). In this scripture, Jesus has shown us *a day* just like He showed Abraham *a day — He showed us a corporate resurrection day.* Since I see and believe in that day, can I receive the fruit of that day through a personal rapturous encounter with Christ? I believe the answer is yes.

> When Abraham, David, and Jesus used time to access the eternal truths of Christ before He was crucified, buried, and resurrected, they set a precedent we can apply and follow.

Just like Abraham did not have to wait to receive the body and the blood of Jesus to affect his body. Just like the psalmist did not have to wait and rejoiced and was glad in the same day Abraham embraced and rejoiced over. Just like David did not have to wait to receive the bread of life, or for the corporate outpouring of the Holy Spirit in Acts 2 for his tabernacle to filled with the glory of God. Just like Jesus did not have to wait for the cross to heal out of His finished work, forgive sin, or raise the dead, we do not have to wait for the things God says are coming at His return. By faith and a revelation of the person of Christ and His eternal day, we can see Him as He is. When we see Him as He is, we use time to access and bring into time, into the earth, and into our lives under heaven, all God has made available in heaven, in eternity, and in Christ — *now*. It is time, it is eternity, *it is a merger.*

12 : TIME AND ETERNITY

CHAPTER 13: THY KINGDOM COME

To say God is merging heaven and earth and time and eternity, is to say He is merging the Kingdom of heaven with the kingdoms of earth through people who live in both places. Revelation 11:15 makes that abundantly clear, "The kingdoms of this world have become the kingdoms of our Lord and of His Christ, and He shall reign forever and ever." It is clearly God's intent that His heavenly rule extend to encompass the kingdoms of this world and He will do it with and through us. The best way for it to be on earth as it is in heaven is to find someone who lives in both places; we live in both places. From the moment God gave mankind dominion, He has never ceased to partner with us for anything He desires to do on earth. He is not going to change that now. The Kingdom will come through us when we see it through a revelation of Christ, carry it, and release it into the earth.

Jesus was, and is, Kingdom-centric. We often think Jesus focused on founding and building His church; that is not true. Jesus founded the church, but He did not overly focus on it. He only used the word "church" (*ecclesia*) twice in the gospels. Once in Matthew 16:18, "*and upon this rock, I will build My church.*" Then again in Matthew 18:15-17, when He said, "*but if he refuses even to hear the church.*" These are the only two times Jesus mentioned the church.

As we have said previously, all things consist in Christ and nothing that was made was made apart from Him. Jesus, who was the Word made flesh and the Word that made everything, told us how to pray, "*Your Kingdom come, Your will be done on earth as it is in heaven*" (Matthew 6:10). Of all the things the Creator of all things could have told us to pray, He told us to pray that our Father's Kingdom would come and His will would be done on earth as it is in heaven. He did not mention the church, salvation, healing, deliverance, ministry, or anything else. Those things were His responsibility and He would manifest them through us in our relationship with Him in the coming of the Kingdom.

> Pray for the Kingdom and the will of God to be in the earth as it is in heaven. Make God your source. Forgive others to be forgiven. Stay aligned with the Kingdom of God and not the Kingdoms of this world and their glory.

Jesus made *His priority* very clear to us: the coming of the Father's Kingdom and will on earth as it is in heaven, which in turn brings wholeness to every area of life. The Lord's Prayer can be summed up in this: Pray for the Kingdom and the will of God to be in the earth as it is in heaven, make God your source, forgive others to be forgiven, and stay aligned with the Kingdom of God and not the kingdoms of this world and their glory. His focus was much different than our focus today.

Today, we focus on building the local church Jesus said He would build. We focus on building ministries, building churches, building buildings and building mailing and donor lists when we should be focused on building the people God sends to us. God does not send His people to us so they can serve us. He sends His people to us so we can serve them with the gifts He has graced us to be as they partner with us.

I know we must honor those in the five-fold ministry. But we can also carry that too far. As five-fold ministers, we are gifts God gave to them to help them fulfill their destinies; they are not gifts, God sent to us to help us fulfill ours. God did not place the five-fold ministry in the church to be served by people. We need to stop thinking about our ministry and start thinking about the destinies of the people God sends to us. He gifted us with those office assignments to serve people and to mature them into the fullness of the measure of the stature of Christ. The fullness of the measure of the stature of Christ *is sonship* (Ephesians 4:9-13).

13 : THY KINGDOM COME

We are called to teach them to hear from God themselves so they can fulfill their purpose; not teach them to serve us so we can fulfill ours. I know this may sound harsh, but our job is to mature people until they no longer need us as their tutors; not to keep them in service to our ministries to ensure our own longevity or job security.

Furthermore, it seems we have made the church Jesus founded an earthly organization that adapts to what it sees and hears on earth to reach those on earth. We are not called to adapt to what we hear and see on earth; we are called to release on earth what we see and hear in heaven. Jesus said He would build His church and we need to let Him. We need to stop being leaders in ministry and become followers in the Kingdom. Jesus did not lead; He followed.

> Jesus was not a leader, He was a follower; it's just that no one could see who He was following.

Jesus was not a leader, He was a follower; it's just that no one could see who He was following. No one could see the Father. Jesus said, "Most assuredly, I say to you, the Son can do nothing of Himself, but what He sees the Father do, for whatever He does, the Son also does in like manner" (John 5:19). Jesus was not a self-initiator based on earthly circumstances or needs. In fact, there were times He walked away from people in need rather than towards them. He did not operate out of what He saw on earth. He demonstrated obedience to reveal His Father's Kingdom and will on earth as His Father in Heaven revealed it to Him.

The problem most of us have is that we cannot see what the Father in heaven is doing so we self-initiate on earth. I have been guilty of this myself. We need to be honest with each other; for the most part, we try to duplicate what we see and what has been modeled for us. We embrace and walk out good ideas. "It worked for them, so maybe it will work for us." We get our vision from what our denomination or spiritual camp is doing, or perhaps from what the pastor down the street is doing. We get our vision from demographics, seminars, conferences, and best business practices. We forgo or adapt Kingdom culture to mirror what we think multiple generations of earthly cultures are looking for. They are changing us; we are not changing them. I understand that we cannot look like Quakers today if we are going to reach this generation. But looking like today's culture is not what is going to win them. Following Christ and revealing His Kingdom will be the most attractive thing we can insert into this present-day culture. We do not lead people to Christ; *they follow us to Him.*

If we insist on using the term "leader" let's not use the "lead from behind" mantra. It is not leading from behind; it is following *from the front.* We must understand that a true Kingdom leader is someone who realizes that they are a king amongst other kings, not a king over a world or ministry filled with others sent to them to fulfill their own personal destiny or vision.

> If we get our vision from the earth, it will only be on earth as it already is on earth.

Then we ask, "How do we reach them?" The answer is simple; by releasing on earth what we see in heaven. We seem to have it backwards; if we get our vision from the earth, it will only be on earth as it already is on earth and *the church will look like everything else on earth.* We are not called to lead them consistent with earthly culture; we are called to follow Christ *from the front* so they can follow us *to Him and His Kingdom.* I am not at all opposed to having contemporary worship services, contemporary platforms, or stage lighting, etc. In fact, I prefer them. I am not averse to those things or modern methods. I am talking about a mindset that is more concerned with culture than Kingdom and more focused on modern methodologies than the leading of the Spirit.

The church is not a threat to the principality in an area when we think like the principality in the area. We are only a threat when we get our vision from above and beyond the reach of principalities, powers, rulers of darkness, and spiritual wickedness in heavenly places. Most cultures reflect the mindset of that geographical area. Many times, the principality in that region is the source of that mindset and resulting lifestyle. If we continually adapt to a culture established by a principality through the populous of a region, we are simply perpetuating that culture with a Christian flavor. That *is not* the Kingdom of God. That is the church trying to be relevant in an earthly culture. If we continually adapt to the culture, then we are being led by the culture, not by the Spirit of God.

The Kingdom message has always been God's priority; it was clearly on His heart before

13 : THY KINGDOM COME

Jesus even began His ministry. John the Baptist preached "Repent for the Kingdom of heaven is at hand" (Matthew 3:2). Then, when Jesus emerged from the wilderness and His temptations, He preached the same message; "*Repent for the Kingdom of heaven is at hand*" (Matthew 4:17). Then, Jesus taught in the synagogues and preached the gospel of the Kingdom.

Jesus begins and closes the Beatitudes with, "*for theirs is the Kingdom of heaven*" (Matthew 5:3,10). After teaching and preaching the gospel of the Kingdom, He tells us how and what to pray: that our Father's Kingdom would come and His will be done on earth as it is in heaven (Matthew 6:10). But He is not through yet. He goes on to say, "seek first the Kingdom of God and His righteousness" (Matthew 6:33). Furthermore, He goes on to teach in parables throughout the Gospels beginning with this statement, "*The Kingdom of heaven is like...*"

If that is not enough, after His death, burial, and resurrection, He presented Himself alive and spoke to them of things pertaining to the Kingdom of God (Acts 1:3). Lastly, Revelation 11:15 says, "The kingdoms of this world have become the Kingdoms of our Lord and His Christ and He shall reign forever and ever." Do you think, perhaps, that Jesus was and is Kingdom-centric? Why was Jesus Kingdom-centric and not church-centric? Because the church belongs to Him and it is His responsibility to build it. He is the chief architect and builder. But the earth is not yet filled with our Father's Kingdom or will. God's Kingdom is supposed to be released through us as our priority the same way it is His priority. He is not speaking to us about His responsibility to build the church; He is speaking to us about our responsibility to reveal our Father's Kingdom on earth as it is in heaven.

If it is His priority, then it should be ours as well. Jesus builds the church, we are the church He builds through relationship with us, and we release the Kingdom that is revealed through a mutual indwelling of God in man and man in Christ. When I say, "the church", I am not talking about an organization or the building on the corner. I am referring to a living, breathing, divine community that is limitless in scope and that envelops the earth through believers. We are called to release the Kingdom that comes through a revelation of Christ and all that is in Him.

The temptations of Jesus in comparison with the Lord's Prayer are clear and powerful demonstration of how we are to function as sons of God in the earth to successfully engage and release our Father's Kingdom. We will briefly discuss the first two temptations and then focus more heavily on the third temptation for our Kingdom alignment. All so it can be on earth as it is in heaven through us. As we discuss the temptations, view each of them according to their context. The context of the first temptation is *personal*, the context of the second temptation is *community*, and the context of the third temptation is *Kingdom*.

Have you ever noticed that the first temptation of Jesus was to turn stones into bread and the first petition of the Lord's Prayer is that God would give us our daily bread? The Lord's Prayer is the model for our successful journey through life's ongoing struggles and temptations. The prayer reveals exactly how Jesus was successful in His encounter with the tempter in the wilderness and throughout His life and ministry in the earth. Look at the chart on the next page to compare the temptations, the Lord's Prayer, and the context of each.

13 : THY KINGDOM COME

Jesus and the Temptations Matthew 4:1–11	The Lord's Prayer Matthew 6:9–13	Context
1. Jesus prayed in the wilderness.	**1.** He told us to pray our Father's Kingdom would come and that His will would be done on earth as it is in heaven.	**1.** Prayer to merge heaven and earth.
2. Turn stones into bread	**2.** Give us this day our daily bread.	**2.** A personal relationship with God as our daily source.
3. Cast yourself down from the temple and angels will bear you up.	**3.** Forgive our debts as we forgive our debtors.	**3.** Community relationships and forgiveness
4. Bow down and worship me and I will give you all the kingdoms of this world and their glory.	**4.** Lead us not into temptation and deliver us from the evil one; for Yours is the Kingdom, the power, and the glory forever. Amen.	**4.** Alignment with the Kingdom of Heaven and not the kingdoms of this world.

Number one in the chart is prayer. First, Jesus spent 40-days in the wilderness and in the heavens in prayer. Then in the Lord's Prayer, He tells us to pray that our Father's Kingdom would come and His will would be done on earth as it is in heaven. The parallel here is that Jesus went into the wilderness to pray and He told us to pray. Not only did He tell us to pray, He made it easy on us and told us what to pray: that our Father's Kingdom would come and His will would be done on earth as it is in heaven. *It was His priority.*

When Jesus was tempted by the devil, He was asked to prove His Sonship by turning the stones into bread. Jesus then tells us to pray that God would give us our daily bread. *That means God is to be our source and supply, not self.* The context is personal. Next, the devil tempted Jesus to jump off the temple and to have angels rescue Him. But in the Lord's Prayer, Jesus tells us to ask God to forgive us as we forgive others. The comparison of the first temptation and the first petition of the Lord's Prayer is obvious — they both speak of bread. That is not the case with the second temptation and the second petition, but the parallel is still clearly there.

If we combine the second temptation and the Lord's Prayer, we will find there are four elements to discuss: death, the temple, rescue by angels, and forgiveness. The devil tempted Jesus to jump towards His death from the temple and to have angels rescue Him. What does that have to do with forgiveness, you ask? Everything. Even though the temple was going to be involved in His death, it was not jumping from the temple that was going to kill Jesus. It was those who were in it; *the community of Christ would be the ones who orchestrated His death, not the temple building.* Jesus would have to forgive them. The context is community.

Next, we see the mention of angels in the temptation, "*He will give His angels charge over you, in their hands they shall bear you up lest you dash your foot against a stone.*" When Jesus left the Garden of Gethsemane, the temple guards came to arrest Him. So now we have the temple involved in His arrest just like the temple was involved in the temptation. But even further, when Peter cut off the ear of the temple guard Jesus said, "*Or do you think that I cannot now pray to My Father, and He will provide Me with more than twelve legions of angels*" (Matthew 26:53)? Here in the garden we have the temple guards arresting Jesus and the possibility of angels rescuing Him to prevent His death. The same scenario we find in the second temptation. But just like Jesus would not jump from the pinnacle of the temple and call upon angels to rescue Him, He did not call angels to rescue Him from the temple guards to prevent the very purpose of His incarnation.

So, the question is, what does "*forgive our sins as we forgive those who sin against us*" have to do with the second temptation? Even when He was being tempted, Jesus knew the temple community would be involved in His death and He would have to forgive them.

Jesus had just come from 40-days with His Father and clearly knew His purpose involved His death at the hands of the earthly priesthood from the temple. While on the cross Jesus said, "Father, forgive them, for they do not know what they do" (Luke 23:34). The first thing Jesus said after revealing the Lord's Prayer is very important. "For if you forgive men their trespasses, your heavenly Father will also forgive you. But if you do not forgive men their trespasses, neither will your Father forgive your trespasses" (Matthew 6:14-15).

Jesus took upon Himself the trespass of all of mankind; therefore, He had to follow the same heavenly protocol of forgiveness as we do. Jesus had to forgive the sins of His community and the sins of the world to redeem His community and the world. He had to forgive so He could condemn and abolish in His flesh, and by His own blood, sin and the separation of Jew and Gentile to make one new forgiven body out of the two (Ephesians 2:13-18).

Jesus made it clear that if we do not forgive, we cannot be forgiven. That applied to Him as well. What did Jesus need to be forgiven of? He did not need forgiveness for His sins; He needed forgiveness for our sins. He became our sin, then forgave us for the sin He became when the priesthood from the temple put Him to death. He forgave for us, and as us, so we could be forgiven and righteous. As the instrument of God's forgiveness, He had to forgive.

> For He made Him who knew no sin to be sin for us,
> that we might become the righteousness of God Him.
> 2 Corinthians 5:21

We must follow the same pattern as Jesus in the first two temptations; we must always keep God as our source and we must always walk in forgiveness towards others to receive forgiveness ourselves. It is not that sin cancels our salvation; when we sin, we enter into agreement with the shadow of death that activates the memory of the body of sin. When we activate the memory of the body of sin, the life of God cannot flow through that memory. That memory usurps our partnership with God, His Kingdom, the law of the Spirit of life in Christ, and relegates us to walk in the lesser works.

Lastly, we will talk about the third temptation, its impact on the church today, and the coming of God's Kingdom through us. The last temptation was: bow down and worship me and I will give you the kingdoms of this world and their glory. The last part of the Lord's Prayer is, "Lead us not into temptation; deliver us from the evil one, for Yours is the Kingdom, the power, and the glory forever. Amen." Jesus said, "Lead us not into temptation and deliver us from the evil one." Where did that come from? I believe it came from His own experience when He was led into the wilderness to be tempted by the evil one. Furthermore, Jesus said, *"For Yours is the Kingdom, the power and the glory."*

In the last temptation, the enemy offered Jesus the kingdoms of this world and their glory; *he did not offer power.* But in the Lord's Prayer Jesus said, "*For Yours is the Kingdom, the power, and the glory.*" The kingdoms of this world take power from you, but the Kingdom of God comes with, and gives power. The context of the third temptation is "kingdom".

You can always tell which system you are operating out of by who retains the power. While the devil offered Jesus the kingdoms and their glory, he never offered Him power. *The Kingdom of God empowers people; the kingdoms of this world take power from people to benefit self.* And yes, that includes church leadership when they exploit churchgoers to build their own kingdoms and ministries, instead of building the people as they have been gifted and called to do.

The enemy wanted to bring the power of God that Jesus carried into his worldly kingdoms and into servitude to increase his own power. He tries to do the same thing with us. He uses us to accomplish his agendas when we align ourselves with man's way of doing things rather than God's. Unlike the world, God does not take power from us; He freely gives it to us.

And you shall remember the Lord your God, for it is He who gives you *power* to get wealth, that He may establish His covenant which He swore to your fathers, as it is this day (Deuteronomy 8:18; emphasis added). Behold, I send the Promise of My Father upon you; but tarry in the city of Jerusalem until you are endued with *power* from on high (Luke

13 : THY KINGDOM COME

24:49; emphasis added). For God has not given us a spirit of fear, but of *power*, and of love, and of a sound mind (2 Timothy 1:7; emphasis added).

Just like God poured out His Spirit on all flesh, God has endued all of humanity with the power to choose. The enemy uses our power to choose to gain access to the power of God we release through our choices. We choose how and where we apply that power. We can use it to engage and express God's Kingdom and will on earth, or we can use it for our own purposes to knowingly or unknowingly further the work of the enemy. We further the work of the enemy by improving and empowering the kingdoms of this world to receive their glory. Jesus declined that offer in favor of the Kingdom of God. Jesus declined the kingdoms of this world and their glory to embrace our Father and His Kingdom.

We can only be truly empowered by God and His Kingdom. We cannot be empowered by a religious system, by the world, or by self-serving leaders. For the most part, the church has accepted the temptation Jesus declined. In so doing, we have transferred the power God gave us to the system that controls us. That is what Christians are doing when they forego their own destinies to serve a single person's vision or when they vote politics instead of being led by the Spirit. We have divested ourselves of God's power by giving it to the leaders of religious institutions and to the worldly systems we live in. We think we are making a righteous choice; but when we repeatedly give our power to any system, that system ultimately limits our options and takes away the power God gave us — the power to choose for ourselves.

We cannot walk in power when we have given that power away like Esau gave away his birthright. God, in His sovereignty, will not override our sovereign power to choose. The kingdoms of this world take power away by using the power we have already given them to limit our choices to the options they make available. The lesser of two evils, we say. When a system retains power, the system wins no matter what options it makes available. Why do we allow the system to offer us two evils? When the system offers two evils, *they have forced us to use our power to choose evil.*

If the church does not break its ties to the kingdoms of this world and their glory, we will continue to be irrelevant and become even more powerless. There is a grace on the church today to exit the system and to enter and operate in the power of the Kingdom of

God. When we do, we will have the power of God to release His Kingdom and to displace the Kingdoms of this world. God does not want us to fix the kingdoms of this world. He wants us to merge them with His Kingdom as sons who see what our Father in heaven is doing so we can do it on earth. "The kingdoms of this world have become the kingdoms of our Lord and of His Christ, and He shall reign forever and ever" (Revelation 11:15). "Most assuredly, I say to you, the Son can do nothing of Himself, but what He sees the Father do; for whatever He does, the Son also does in like manner" (John 5:19).

It is not our place to war against the current systems; it is our job to create a Kingdom environment that will draw people into it and away from current world systems. Buckminster Fuller, an American poet, philosopher, inventor, and mathematician once said, "You never change things by fighting the existing reality. To change something, build a new model that makes the existing model obsolete."[7] I fully concur with that statement, what a thought. When we release and reveal the Kingdom of God, people will leave the existing systems and migrate to the Kingdom we have released on earth as it is in heaven. That is what Jesus told us to pray for.

The church is hurting today. It is hemorrhaging people at an alarming rate. Why? Because people have grown tired of the current church model; they are not interested in going around the mountain again. It is time to leave the wilderness of church-as-usual to enter the Promised Land of Kingdom realities. Adapting to the culture does not make the church relevant. It simply means the church is trying to stay with the times instead of setting the pace and releasing eternal Kingdom realities into time.

In my international travels, I have encountered a significant number of people dissatisfied with the current state of the church. They want more of God than comes across the pulpit. They want everything Jesus died to give and make them; not another message based on living a good life through spiritual principles. We want and need more.

As sons of our Father in heaven, we have been given the opportunity and honor to reveal God and His Kingdom. We are not here to fight the existing model of the church or the world; we are here to introduce the Kingdom of God to a fallen world that was built

---

[7] https://www.goodreads.com/author/quotes/11515303.R_Buckminster_Fuller

13 : THY KINGDOM COME

on a self-serving, sinful paradigm and fallen genetics. As we said earlier, the world system is built on a blood-based foundation of fallen genetics. We must choose to build on the blood-bought redemptive foundation of the blood of Jesus. Both systems are in operation in the earth and the church must choose which system to build on: God's or man's, the rock or the sand.

The Kingdom of God is built on the rock, a foundation of stone, the foundation stone with the blood of the Lamb (Isaiah 28:16). The world builds on the sand, the sand that opened its mouth to receive the blood of Abel (Matthew 7:24-27). If we build our life on God's thoughts (sayings) and His ways, we are building on the rock, on a sure foundation. But if we build our life on the thoughts and ways of the world (if we build on cultural adaptations, the basic principles of the world and the traditions of men) we are building on the sand. When we build on the sand of world systems, it will not last even if it is spiritually motivated with scriptural quotations. We must be in the culture but not of it. Jesus only did what He saw His Father do and He had the most successful "ministry" the world has ever seen. The Father has given us the assignment to release His Kingdom as an ongoing expression of Christ and His destiny because we are the body of Christ.

As believers in Jesus, we have always known that we are to pray for our Father's Kingdom and His will to be on earth as it is in heaven. We can no longer focus on building ministries or our own kingdoms in the name of God. We should rethink the modern idea of "ministry" to embrace the reality of Kingdom. How do we do that? It begins with seeing the Kingdom.

CHAPTER 14: SEEING THE KINGDOM

Up to this point, we have focused on God's desire for His Kingdom to be on earth as it is in heaven. Now, we will focus on *seeing the Kingdom* He wants on earth as it is in heaven. In John's Gospel, Jesus told Nicodemus, "*Most assuredly, I say to you, unless one is born from above, he cannot see the Kingdom of God*" (John 3:3). Jesus said we cannot see the Kingdom if we are not born from above. Why can we not see the Kingdom if we are not born from above? Because the Kingdom is in Christ and if we are not born from above, we cannot enter and abide in Christ where the Kingdom abides. This also means if we *are* born from above, we *can* see the Kingdom because we are in Christ where the Kingdom abides. We see the Kingdom that abides in Christ through a revelation of the person of Christ. Why will a revelation of Christ result in our seeing the Kingdom? Our answer lies in Paul's letter to the Colossians.

> *For by Him all things were created that are in heaven and that are on earth, visible and invisible, whether thrones or dominions or principalities or powers.* All things were created through Him and for Him. And He is before all things, *and in Him, all things consist.* And He is the head of the body, *the church*, who is the beginning, the firstborn from the dead, that in all things He may have the preeminence. Colossians 1:16–19 (emphasis added)

In this passage, Paul makes it clear all things created, in heaven and on the earth, visible or invisible, were created by Him and in Him all things consist. All things consist in Him. Everything is in Christ. Our discovery of Christ and all things created *is in Christ*. We can choose to view this passage as figurative or strictly positional, but that lessens the truth and reality of what Paul is trying to teach us, that all things were created by and exist in Christ. That does not mean the fallen world is in Christ. It means we are in Christ where all things are reconciled and where everything Kingdom abides.

The substance of every Kingdom event is in Christ. The substance of every Kingdom strategy is in Christ. The wisdom of the Kingdom is in Christ. Everything we need to release the Kingdom on earth can be found in the Kingdom, in Christ. Speaking of the Father and Christ, Paul said, "In whom are hidden all the treasures of wisdom and knowledge," and speaking of Christ, "For in Him we live, and move, and have our being." (Colossians 2:3, Acts 17:28)

> Our life is a journey through Christ, not a journey through time.

Paul said we live in Him, move in Him, and have our being in Him. That is why I believe *our lives are a journey through Christ, not a journey through time*. We are literally alive in Christ and our journey is an ongoing revelation of Christ. It is a journey of discovery. It is a revelation of who we are in Him as members of His spiritual and incarnate body. It is a revelation of the Kingdom and the realms and dimensions that exist within Him. To see the Kingdom is to receive a revelation of Christ, the King of the Kingdom.

If you have Bible software or a concordance, do a search of the phrase "in Christ." You will be amazed at how many times that phrase appears and what it reveals about what is in Him. Paul said that he was caught up and saw things that were *unlawful for a man to utter*. We must conclude then, that he wrote what he was permitted to share, and withheld the things he was not. The fact that all things are "in Christ" is one of the things he saw and was permitted and called to share. *Paul revealed the "in Christ" realities of his "in Christ" experiences* (2 Corinthians 12:4). "In Christ" is the true location of our being, not merely a positional, unattainable truth — it is just that we must become consciously aware of our true surroundings.

14 : SEEING THE KINGDOM

We said this in Chapter 11: "We cannot neglect our role in the coming of God's Kingdom and will into the earth. The present kingdoms of this world were not formed by pre-fall Adam in partnership with God. They were formed after the fall by fallen mankind; they do not look like heaven or God's plan for the earth. That is why Jesus told us to pray that our Father's Kingdom would come and His will would be done on earth as it is in heaven. It is not on earth as it is in heaven, and it will not be if we continue to get our vision from the earth." We must get our vision from heaven, not the earth. All things in the reconciled heavens and earth are in Christ; therefore, we must have a revelation of Him and a revelation of the Kingdom within Him.

I mentioned previously that one of the two places Jesus spoke of the church was in Matthew 16:13-20. What is interesting about this passage is that Jesus also mentioned the Kingdom. It is the only passage where Jesus mentions both the church and the Kingdom. In fact, Jesus did not merely mention the Kingdom, He said He would give us the keys to the Kingdom. Let's look at the conversation where Jesus asked His disciples, "*But who do you say that I am?*" Peter answered and said,

> "You are the Christ, the Son of the living God." Jesus answered and said to him, *"Blessed are you, Simon Bar-Jonah, for flesh and blood has not revealed this to you, but my Father who is in heaven.* And I also say to you that you are Peter, and on this rock I will build My church, and the gates of Hades shall not prevail against it. And I will give you the keys of the Kingdom of heaven, and whatever you bind on earth will be bound in heaven, and whatever you loose on earth will be loosed in heaven."
> (Matthew 16:16-20) (emphasis added)

In this passage, Jesus mentioned the church and the keys of the Kingdom. But before He mentioned either, He told Peter he was blessed because he *received a revelation* that He was the Christ and then added, "*...on this rock, I will build my church.*" It is important to notice why Jesus said Peter was blessed. "Blessed are you, Simon Bar-Jonah, *for flesh and blood has not revealed this to you, but My Father who is in heaven.*" Jesus did not say Peter was blessed because he knew He was the Christ; He said Peter was blessed because he did not receive the revelation from men on earth, *but from His Father in heaven.* Jesus called Peter blessed because he received a revelation of Christ from God in heaven, not from men on earth.

If the church was founded on receiving a revelation of Christ from heaven, it will be built on a continued revelation of Christ from heaven. A building must be aligned with the shape of the foundation for it to stand. The "rock" the church is built on is Christ Himself with a two-fold reality: the revelation that Jesus is the Christ, the Son of the living God, *and on people...people who are the church and hear from our Father in heaven.* Jesus will build His church the same way He founded His church: through people who hear from heaven to receive a revelation of who He is *and* all that is in Him.

Jesus is the central figure in the creation because everything within the creation is centered in Him. He is the Word of God. Nothing that has been made was made apart from Him; all things are in Him. That means the keys of the Kingdom of heaven open doors to the Kingdom that are in Christ wherein all things consist. What do the keys open? They open the revelation that Christ has of Himself; they grant access to all things made by Him and all realms and dimensions that exist in Him. Jesus said the Kingdom of God is within us, if it is within us, *it is also within Christ* (Luke 17:20).

> The keys of the kingdom of heaven unlock deeper revelations of Christ Himself. They open every kingdom thing and every kingdom realm that is in Christ and in us through the mutual indwelling of God in man and man in Christ.

It is important to note that Jesus said the keys were to the Kingdom of heaven. Rattling the keys to the Kingdom of heaven at the gates of hell does absolutely nothing to stop hell. It has no more benefit or impact than rattling the keys to your home at your neighbor's home. The keys have nothing to do with hell, but everything to do with the Kingdom of heaven that resides within Christ and within us. Jesus then said that whatever we bind on earth is bound in heaven, and whatever we loose on earth is loosed in heaven. The revelation of Christ we receive and become one with when we use the keys to open a door, a realm, or a revelation in Him, is what brings binding and loosing into powerful action in our lives.

Jesus told Peter that he would bind and loose. If there are two people that should know about binding and loosing, it is Jesus and Peter. Yet, I find no scriptural record of Jesus or Peter binding and loosing the way many practice it today. *"I bind you, I loose you."* Binding and loosing the devil is like rattling the keys of the Kingdom at the gates of hell. You may say, "Well, it works for me!" My response would be, "Be it unto you according to your faith." You do have authority as a believer and your faith is released through your words and your actions, but that does not mean the way we practice binding and loosing is consistent with scripture.

Jesus told Peter he would bind and loose and that heaven and earth would be united when he did. Binding and loosing is one aspect of making it on earth as it is in heaven. Notice Jesus did not mention hell, hades, demons, spirits, sickness or death; He mentioned heaven and earth when it came to binding and loosing. When Jesus did mention the gates of hell/hades, He said the gates of hell would not prevail against the church He was building, a church that knew who He was and was positioned to hear and receive revelation from heaven. The gates of hell will not prevail against the church when it hears from heaven like Peter did.

What is it then to bind and loose? Binding and loosing is the process whereby God unites heaven and earth because someone on earth accessed the Kingdom of heaven in Christ through His indwelling presence. He was telling Peter that when he used the keys of the Kingdom to unlock and discover a greater and ongoing revelation of Christ, and His Kingdom, it would bind the work of the enemy on earth because of his encounter with what was *already* bound or loosed in heaven. What did it look like when Peter bound and loosed? It looked like Peter walking past a crowd and people being healed by his shadow. Peter did not say a word; he did not bind, loose, or even speak (Acts 15:5).

What Peter encountered in the Kingdom was finished in the Kingdom to become an authority he carried and released. That authority was active and effectively *loosed the Kingdom within him* to touch those around him who were infirmed. What did Peter encounter in the Kingdom? I submit that he encountered and received a deeper revelation of Christ and then became the living expression of that revelation — he became an incarnate expression of Christ. Jesus called Peter blessed because he received a revelation from heaven. He then gave him the keys to the Kingdom so he could be built up as the church to receive more revelation from heaven. There is a difference between the Peter in Matthew 16 who received a revelation that Jesus was the Christ, and the Peter in Acts 15 who carried the Jesus he had a revelation of. The Peter in Matthew 16 was blessed to hear from the

Father and to receive a revelation from Him. The Peter in Acts 15 met and expressed the Father, Christ, and the Kingdom through a deeper level of revelation and relationship.

Jesus told us this relationship was coming in John 14. John 14 is all about relationship and the indwelling presence of God that results in a revelation of Christ.

> Let not your heart be troubled; you believe in God, believe also in Me. In My Father's house are many mansions; if it were not so, I would have told you. I go to prepare a place for you. And if I go and prepare a place for you, I will come again and receive you to Myself; that where I am, there you may be also. And where I go you know, and the way you know. Thomas said to Him, "Lord, we do not know where You are going, and how can we know the way?" Jesus said to him, "I am the way, the truth, and the life. No one comes to the Father except through Me." John 14:1-6

John 14 is a relational chapter. I am sorry if this disappoints you, but it has nothing to do with Jesus building us a mansion in heaven. Let's start by breaking this passage down. First, Jesus said, "Let not your heart be troubled; you believe in God, believe also in Me." Jesus was telling them to transfer the template of their belief in God onto Him. The next thing Jesus said was, "In My Father's house are many mansions; if it were not so, I would have told you." The subject is now the Father's house.

We must recognize that Jesus was His Father's house at the time He made that statement. Jesus made it clear that His Father was in Him and that He was the way to the Father. The word "mansions" in Greek is the word *"monai"* which means a dwelling place or abode. Jesus was saying there are many dwelling places within Him to dwell. That is why we can now abide in Him. His very next statement makes that very clear: "I go to prepare a place for you. And if I go and prepare a place for you, I will come again and *receive you to Myself.*"

Jesus said He was going to prepare a place for us so He could receive us to *Himself.* The time of His death was rapidly approaching and His death was at the heart of His conversation with His disciples. Jews believed that when you died and were of the faith of Abraham, you went to Abraham's bosom. Jesus was declaring that He was not going to a place, but that He was going to *become the place.* He was saying that He was not going to Abraham's bosom, but that we are going to His bosom just like He was in the bosom of the Father (John 1:18). He would receive us to Himself so we could abide in Him where the

Kingdom is and where all things are reconciled. A person had to die to go to Abraham's bosom and we have died to abide in Christ. When we accepted Christ, we were baptized into his death, burial, and resurrection. We have died and now abide in Him where all things Kingdom abide.

Jesus made it clear He was going back to His Father so that we could abide in Him and in the Father. Jesus later said in verse 23, "If anyone loves Me, He will keep My Word, and My Father will love Him, and we will come to Him and make our home with Him." The word "home" in verse 23 is the same word used for mansions in verse 2, "*monai*." If Jesus was saying that He was going to prepare a mansion *for us*, then He was also saying that He and the Father are going to make a mansion *in us*.

In verse 20, Jesus said, "At that day you will know that I am in My Father, and you in Me, and I in you." It is abundantly clear, the entire context of the passage in John 14 is about relationship and the impending mutual indwelling presence; God in man and man in Christ. Furthermore, Jesus said, "He who has My commandments and keeps them, it is he who loves Me. And he who loves Me will be loved by My Father, and I will love him and manifest Myself to him" (John 14:21). Jesus said He would manifest (*disclose and reveal*) Himself to us, that is a revelation of His person and all that is in Him. Jesus continued with the same relational theme in John 15:5 when He said, "I am the vine, you are the branches. He who abides in Me, and I in him, bears much fruit; for without Me you can do nothing."

Not only did Jesus let us know of the mutual indwelling of He and His Father, He also said Holy Spirit would dwell in us. "The Spirit of truth, whom the world cannot receive because it neither sees Him nor knows Him; but you know Him, for He dwells with you and will be in you" (John 14:17). The Apostle John wrote the Gospel of John, the Books of 1, 2, and 3 John, and the Book of Revelation. He had a revelation of Christ. John understood that one purpose of the indwelling was to teach us about abiding in Christ.

> But the anointing which you have received from Him *abides in you*,
> and you do not need that anyone teach you; but as the same anointing
> *teaches you concerning all things*, and is true, and is not a lie,
> and just as it has taught you, *you abide in Him*.
> 1 John 2:27 (emphasis added)

God has merged with man to reveal Himself *to* man and God has merged with man to reveal Himself *through* man. We are in Him and He is in us through a mutual indwelling. The outworking of the merger of God and man is a process whereby we walk in an ever-increasing revelation of Christ, to reveal Christ, because we are His body. It is a journey through every realm and dimension of the Kingdom that exists within Christ so we can carry and release what we see there into the earth.

How do we see the Kingdom? We see the Kingdom through a revelation of the King of the Kingdom — Jesus. We see the Kingdom through a personal, intimate, and ongoing revelation of Christ and all that is in Him. Our lives in Christ become a binding and loosing force within the creation. That is what Peter experienced when he was given the keys of the Kingdom and that is what we access and experience when we are given the keys to the Kingdom. The keys to the Kingdom open realms and dimensions in Christ to reveal who He is and all that is in Him. Seeing Christ is seeing the Kingdom; a revelation of Christ is a revelation of the Kingdom.

John had an incredible encounter with Jesus. He received a revelation of Jesus Christ and the realms within Him; we know it as the Book of Revelation. The Book of Revelation is the result of the God in man and man in Christ dynamic. Peter was not the only one given the keys to the Kingdom of heaven leading to a greater revelation of the person of Christ. Like all believers, John had the keys to the Kingdom as well. Let's begin with Revelation 1:1.

> *The Revelation of Jesus Christ, which God gave Him to show His servants* – things which must shortly take place. And *He sent and signified it by His angel to His servant John*, who bore witness to the Word of God, *and to the testimony of Jesus Christ, to all things that he saw.* (emphasis added)

The first thing we see is that the Book of Revelation is a revelation of the person of Jesus Christ and what the Father gave Him. The next thing is that God sent an angel to

14 : SEEING THE KINGDOM

John. That is the merger of the community of heaven and the community of earth for the purposes of revealing Christ and what is in Him. Next, we see that John bore witness to the Word of God and to the testimony of Jesus Christ, *to all things he saw*. John saw and received a revelation of Christ and the Kingdom within Him. How did he see the Kingdom within Him?

> Behold, I stand at the *door* and knock. If anyone hears My voice and opens the *door*, I will come into him and dine with him, and he with Me. To him who overcomes I will grant to sit with Me on My throne, as I also overcame and sat down with My Father on His throne. He who has ears to hear, let him hear what the Spirit says to the churches.
> Revelation 3:20-22 (emphasis added)

> After these things I looked, and behold, a *door* standing open in heaven. And the first voice which I heard was like a trumpet speaking with me, saying, "Come up here, and I will show you things which must take place after this."
> Revelation 4:1 (emphasis added)

As we look at Revelation 3 and 4, notice both passages speak of a door. The first door is to our hearts and Jesus is standing at the door and knocking; He is outside of the door and wants to come into fellowship with us. I am not saying Christ does not live in the believer; He does. This is talking about an intimate relationship beyond our new birth. Jesus is more interested in the mutual indwelling than we are. He is the one who initiated relationship with us: "*You did not choose Me; I have chosen you*" (John 15:16). As we read earlier, Jesus said He would manifest Himself to those who love Him. That is what we are witnessing here with John and it is what is available to all of us: fellowship with Christ in the very depths of our hearts.

The second door is in heaven; it is a realm within Christ. He opens His heart to those who open their hearts to Him. Notice first that John heard a voice, just like Adam heard a voice in the garden and just like Jesus heard a voice at His baptism. The voice told John to, "Come up here." Jesus said, "*I am the door*." Jesus is the door that elevated John into the heavens. Jesus elevated John into His heart.

> Most assuredly, I say to you, *I am the door of the sheep.* All who ever came before Me are thieves and robbers, but the sheep did not hear them. *I am the door.* If anyone enters by Me, he will be saved and will go *in and out and find pasture.*
> John 10:7-9 (emphasis added)

Jesus is the door and He said we would go in and out and find pasture. What does it mean to go in and out and find pasture? I believe it means we come in and out of the realms and dimensions within Christ. We go in and out to walk in an ever-increasing revelation of Him so we become one with Him in heaven to release Him on earth as His body. If we abide in Christ, we never leave Christ, we are always in Him. If we never leave Him, how do we go in and out? We go in and out through our deep encounters with Him and then release the Christ and Kingdom we encounter there into the world we are in, but not of. *We change the culture, the culture does not change us.*

Some may say, "It clearly states the door is in heaven, it does not say it is Christ or the heart of Christ." True, but there are three things we have to remember: John's whole encounter was identified as "The Revelation of Jesus Christ" not a revelation of heaven. Everything John saw was a revelation of Christ. Secondly, Jesus said to Himself that He is the door to the sheep. Jesus is the Great Shepherd and John was in His sheepfold and went in and out to find pasture. That is how John received his revelation of Christ and what is in Christ. Thirdly, Paul said, "That in the dispensation of the fullness of the times He might gather together in one all things *in Christ, both which are in heaven and which are on earth — in Him."* Paul made it very clear that all things which are in heaven and which are on earth are *in Him.* John was given access to the heavenly dimensions within Christ to see the Kingdom within Christ.

God does not simply release His Kingdom into the earth; He brings us into the Kingdom within Himself so we can see that Kingdom. The corresponding Kingdom embedded in our very being is activated by relational revelation and released through us in the earth. That is why Jesus stands at the door and knocks. He wants to manifest Himself to us to open the Kingdom within us. When He enters our hearts, He brings all that is *in Him.* He brings the reconciled heavens and earth. He brings the fullness of the Kingdom and He brings the fullness of the Godhead.

14 : SEEING THE KINGDOM

When He enters our hearts and His Kingdom within us to fellowship, He opens His heart to us while in our hearts. Our hearts then enter His heart to see the part of Himself He chooses to manifest, disclose, and reveal to us. Once again, this is all about the God in man, man in Christ dynamic, it is all about relationship: "I go to prepare a place for you. And if I go and prepare a place for you, *I will come again and receive you to Myself.*" That is exactly what He did with John. He received John fully into Himself to see the revelation God gave Him to share with His servants. Jesus was not speaking figuratively when He said we abide in Him. It is a reality that we must engage to encounter Him and all that is in Him. John's encounter with Christ is a revelation of how we are to interact with Christ and what is in Him.

This is another area where I believe the church has missed it. We have lived on the crumbs of scriptural interpretation without becoming that Word made flesh, without realizing the fullness of the spiritual relationship itself. We need both. The scriptures are living and reveal who God is and what He has made available to us in Christ. We must pursue the relational "in Christ" realities of our redemption rather than merely understanding what the scriptures say are in Him and coming to us some day. God is real and so is our relationship with Him. John's encounter is a beautiful demonstration of a life in relationship with Christ and all that it is supposed to be — a revelation of Christ and what is in Him.

Paul repeatedly said everything is in Christ. That includes what John saw when he was caught up and entered through the door that is Christ. What did John see when he entered the door? He saw the revelation the Father gave Jesus (Revelation 1:1). He saw a throne and the twenty-four elders on their thrones. Jesus said, "No one comes to the Father but through Me" (John 14:6). Did you notice that Jesus said, "*through Me*"? John entered "*through the door*" and he saw what was in Christ. This is yet another indication that all we are seeing in John's revelatory encounter *with Christ*, is what is *in Christ*. Paul said,

> For by Him all things were created *that are in heaven* and that are on earth, visible and invisible, *whether thrones* or dominions or principalities or powers. All things were created through Him and for Him. And He is before all things, and *in Him, all things consist.*
> Colossians 1:16–19 (emphasis added)

To our point, Paul mentions three things that apply to John's encounter with Christ, in the heaven that is in Christ: 1. By Him, all things were created that are *in heaven, All things in heaven are in Christ.* 2. *Thrones* are in heaven, and, 3. *In Him all things consist.* What "all things"? *All the things mentioned in this verse*; all things created that are in heaven and on earth were created through Him and for Him, and consist in Him. Everything we see in John's revelatory encounter: heaven, thrones, and the elders are all *in Christ.*

Let's take this one step further. When we talked about the lesser works in Chapter 7, we also talked about the kenosis. That is when Jesus emptied the form of God and took on the form of man. When we discussed it, we asked this question: "What did He empty Himself of?" We answered that question in part. Here is the dilemma, "How can all things be in Him if He emptied Himself?" I believe He emptied Himself of everything John saw in his encounter with Christ; all things that were created through Him and for Him – that is what He left in His Father while He was in the earth. That is why Jesus said, "He will glorify Me, for He will take of what is Mine and declare it to you. All things that the Father has are Mine. Therefore I said that He will take of Mine and declare it to you" (John 16:14-16).

Jesus said Holy Spirit would "take of what is Mine and declare it to you." He also said, "All things the Father has are Mine." Jesus did not say Holy Spirit would share what belonged to the Father, He said He would take what belonged to Him and share it with us. The reason everything the Father has belongs to Jesus is that Jesus who created all things emptied Himself of all things created and left them in His Father. That is why He could say, "All things the Father has are Mine."

When Jesus was baptized by John the Baptist, the heavens were opened to Him. The first thing we see is Jesus receives a word revealing His identity as God's Son; He heard the voice of God. Then, He used time, through prayer, to ascend into His own eternal day to become one with His Father to receive a fuller revelation of Himself. *By the way, John's "come up here" Isle of Patmos wilderness experience was a repeat of Christ's ascension in the wilderness and a demonstration of what is available to us. John was in the Spirit on the Lord's day and ascended — while there, he received a revelation of Jesus Christ.* The revelation Christ received when He ascended into the heavens and into His own eternal day, filled Him with what He previously emptied Himself of. But this time, it was not in Him because He was the Son of God who was in the form of God and equal with God as the Creator of all things. This time, God gave it to the obedient Son of Man as an ongoing progressive revelation of who He was as God before coming to earth. The Son of Man was filled, by revelation, with the very things the Son of God emptied Himself of at His incarnation.

Jesus emptied Himself of all things that were in Him as Creator, to receive it later as a revelation from His Father through relationship. "A revelation you ask?" Yes, a revelation. Do you remember Revelation 1:1? *"The Revelation of Jesus Christ which God gave Him."* When Jesus received the Father within Himself, His Father gave Him a revelation and through that revelation, Jesus received all He left in the Father. It was restored "in Him" as a revelation through His obedience as the Son of Man. When He received the revelation of self He had when He was God, He walked the earth as fully God and fully man. Even so, He kept His identity, all that He was, all that He knew, and all the glory of God hidden in the form of man. As we said in Chapter 8, what Jesus kept hidden was destined for our glory. We are called to reveal what Jesus had to keep veiled.

When Jesus ascended to His Father after His resurrection, He was glorified with the Father the way He had been before the world was created (John 17:5). After His ascension and glorification, everything He created could now be seen in Him and through Him; it was no longer hidden. John entered through the door that is Christ to see things that are in and belong to Christ.

When I was praying one evening, I kept telling the Lord that I wanted relationship with Him and revelation of Him. As I repeated this over and over, I suddenly heard myself say, "I want revelationship with you." When I realized what I said, I was captivated by it. What is revelationship? It is when you have an ongoing cycle of relationship that leads to revelation, which leads to deeper relationship, which leads to deeper revelation, so on and so forth. It is a glorious cycle that results in an ever-increasing level of oneness with Christ. God wants to engage in "*revelationship*" with us.

Our growth in Christ is literally, growth *in Christ*. In Him we live, and move, and have our being. As we engage in ongoing "*revelationship*" with Christ through Holy Spirit, we open realms within our hearts to Him and He opens realms of His heart to reveal Himself and His Kingdom to us. Revelationship is a two-way relationship whereby we engage in fellowship with Christ in our own hearts and with Christ in His heart. Let me restate something I said earlier in this chapter.

> Life is a journey through Christ, not a journey through time.

Any revelation we encounter is in some form or fashion, a revelation of Christ. All things were made by Him and through Him; they are therefore a revelation of Him. We really need to take what Paul said literally, "*In Him we live, and move, and have our being.*" The heart of Christ is the environment of our very existence as new creatures in Christ. It is the environment of Kingdom, revelation, wisdom, knowledge, redemption, restoration, regeneration, and the fulfillment of all God has destined for us. The heart of Christ contains all things Kingdom; all things that belong to Christ the King.

We are called to walk the same path Jesus walked ahead of us. What path is that? It is the "*empty ourselves of self to be refilled with who we are in Christ and who Christ is in us*" path. We engage in our own kenotic process. We empty ourselves of who we know ourselves to be in the earth to be filled with a revelation of our eternal identity and destiny in Christ. We must surrender our lives in the earth through "*revelationship*" to be filled with Christ and who He created us to be. This is so we can fully merge and become one with the glory that was ordained for us.

Our role is to engage a revelation of the truth, to see the Kingdom, all that is in Christ, and to discover who we are in Him. We are in Christ and belong to Christ. If we truly want to "find ourselves" we must go deep into the place where we are hidden, just like Jesus did.

Jesus left Himself in His Father. When He ascended through prayer in the wilderness following His baptism, He entered back into the place He left Himself – into His Father. Likewise, our lives are now *hidden with Christ in God* (Colossians 3:3). If we want to find ourselves, we must go deep into the place we are hidden: in Christ, and in God. Our identity is not in this realm; it is in Christ. This is evidenced in the life of Jeremiah.

> Before I formed you in the womb I knew you. Before you were born I sanctified you; I ordained you a prophet to the nations.
> Jeremiah 1:5

14 : SEEING THE KINGDOM

God said He knew Jeremiah and ordained him a prophet to the nations before He formed him in his mother's womb. God made a specific statement, "*Before I formed you in the womb I knew you.*" He did not say He knew Jeremiah before he was formed in the womb. He said He knew Jeremiah before *He* formed him in the womb. He also said He sanctified him and ordained him a prophet to the nations. When God told Jeremiah that he was a prophet to the nations, Jeremiah received a revelation of his identity in God. God told Jeremiah what He knew about him before he was born. God gave Jeremiah a revelation of his eternal purpose. After God put His word in Jeremiah's mouth, He asked him what he saw. *When Jeremiah received a revelation of his identity in God and received God's word, he saw the Kingdom* (Jeremiah 1:11-13).

When God gives us a glimpse into the lives of others, He is showing us how He operates with us as well. Through Jeremiah, He is showing us that we have been sanctified and ordained for a purpose in Him before we were formed in the womb. We mean that much to God!

Our journey is the same as that of Jeremiah and Christ. When we receive a revelation of Christ, and all that is in Him, we will receive a revelation of the Kingdom and a revelation of who we are because we are the body of Christ in the earth. From that place of relationship and revelation — "*revelationship*" — we will see Christ, the Kingdom, and who we are in and as His body in the earth. It is then that we will be able to properly operate in the Kingdom. When we operate in the Kingdom, we literally engage heaven to bring the heaven we have engaged to earth. We will be the answers to, and the living expression of the Lord's Prayer: "*Your Kingdom come, Your will be done on earth as it is in heaven.*" It will be on earth as it is in heaven through us, because we see, become, and release the Kingdom we see in Christ into the earth.

CHAPTER 15: OPERATING IN THE KINGDOM

To operate in the Kingdom is to create outside of time from within the Creator – we are in Christ. We use time to access eternity and the Kingdom that is outside of time, in Christ, to bring it into time in the earth. To operate in the Kingdom is to see into the heavens within Christ and to co-create with Him from a place where heaven and earth are already reconciled and all things are new. When we create there, we are releasing the new in Christ into the fallen creation. It is the release of God's Kingdom on earth as it is in heaven into the realms and worlds God created and gave man dominion over. God wants us to create worlds within worlds to replace worlds within worlds. Manifest sons are called to manifest worlds.

> Manifest sons are called to manifest worlds.

God created a world for us to live in so we could create a world for Him to live in. Jesus created all things and we abide in Him. It is our nature to create; God loves watching and working with us to create. He created us to co-create with Him and He is teaching and discipling us to create like He creates.

God is our Father and Jesus is our older brother. God receives glory when we partner with Him to create an environment for Him to inhabit with us. When we co-create with God, we are not improving the kingdoms *of this world*, we are releasing the Kingdom of

God *into this world*. Our purpose is not to improve world systems, it is to replace them with the Kingdom of God so God has a Kingdom environment to inhabit in this world with us. Do you remember what Buckminster Fuller said? He said, "*You never change things by fighting the existing reality. To change something, build a new model that makes the existing model obsolete.*" The existing reality equates to the kingdoms of this world built on the foundation established by Cain's sacrifice of Abel. The new model is the Kingdom of God we co-create and release into the earth built on the foundation established by Christ's sacrifice-of-Self.

A part of our problem has been that we engage world systems from within world systems with Kingdom principles. We engage those systems with Kingdom principles and expect the world systems (which operate from a different foundation) to respond to us to provide things only the Kingdom of God can provide. We are not called to operate in the systems of this world. We are called to operate in the Kingdom of God to change this world and its systems. Kingdom principles are not earthly kingdom principles; they are Kingdom of heaven principles.

When we co-create to release the Kingdom of God in the earth, we have created an environment that functions by the very principles we have been endeavoring to apply to the kingdoms of this world; they are two different kingdoms built on two different foundations that were framed with different words. We are called to operate in the Kingdom by seeing the Kingdom; and we are called to build within the Kingdom, to release the Kingdom we have built in, and with Christ, into the earth. The environment within Christ the Creator is a creative environment. We are to abide and create from there. So then, how do we co-create with God? We follow God's creative process; we frame, form and fill.

> God's creative process: Framing – Forming – Filling.

The first step in God's creative process is *framing*.

> By faith, we understand that the worlds were framed by the Word of God,
> so that the things which are seen
> were not made of things which are visible.
> Hebrews 11:3

15 : OPERATING IN THE KINGDOM

The writer of Hebrews makes it abundantly clear that the worlds were framed by the Word of God, and the seen is a visible manifestation of the unseen. That is how God creates and that is how we must create. That is how we frame the worlds that we create within this created world — with the Word of God. Notice I said the "Word of God." We can create with our own words, but world systems and governments have already been framed and created by man's words. That is why we refer to the Foundings Fathers of America as the "Framers of the Constitution." Other examples: myocardial infarction, translating tendency, and lateral weight transfer. What are those? They are words you only understand in the context of the world they frame. A myocardial infarction is a coronary event, a heart attack — *the medical world*. Translating tendency is the tendency of single rotor helicopters to translate laterally due to tail rotor thrust — *the aviation world*. Lateral weight transfer is a term used to describe the lateral shift of weight when a vehicle negotiates a corner — *the driving world*. All three of these terms mean nothing to us unless we are part of the world they frame.

While God wants us to create with words, we are to create with His Words, words that abide in us, the Word of God. We live, move and have our being in Christ and in His Word. That is where we get our vision to create. We speak the Word of God from within the Word of God Himself to create worlds within the created world. Jesus said...

> I am the vine, you are the branches. He who abides in Me, and I in him, bears much fruit; for without Me you can do nothing.
> John 15:5

> If you abide in Me, and My words abide in you, you will ask what you desire, and it shall be done for you. By this My Father is glorified, that you bear much fruit, so you will be My disciples.
> John 15:7-8

In these passages, Jesus continues the theme of John 14, the mutual indwelling of God in man and man in Christ. This mutual indwelling is the source of the fruit we are called to bear. What fruit are we called to bear? An apple tree bears apples as its fruit, a peach tree bears peaches as its fruit, and the Creator bears creation(s) and co-creators as His fruit. Jesus also said the Father is glorified when we bear much fruit and that we are His disciples.

The Creator disciples co-creators to bear much fruit. We referenced Ecclesiastes 3:11 in Chapter 1, we said God placed eternity in the hearts of men. The word for eternity in that passage is "olam." Olam is also translated as *worlds*. God placed worlds in our hearts; I say again, manifest sons are called to manifest worlds. The question is, "How do we manifest those worlds?"

In verse 7, Jesus said, "If you abide in Me." As we have said many times, we abide in Christ. We abide in the Creator of all things so that we can create all things as His disciples, as sons of our Father. Paul said that all things were created through and for Christ so anything we create must follow the "*through and for Christ*" pattern or it is not of God. We cannot create outside of Christ; if we do, it is an illegitimate creation that did not come into being *through and for Christ*. All things were created through Him and for Him, we must follow that pattern, God's method has not and will not change. (Colossians 1:16)

Next, Jesus said, "*and My Words abide in you, you will ask what you desire.*" We abide in Him and His Words abide in us. This is critical to God's creative process. What happens when His Word abides in us? His Word in us becomes a revelation that frames the world He wants us to create through us; *it literally forms a vision in us of the world we are about to co-create through and for Christ.* God first frames a world in us *with His Word* so we can frame a world through and for Him *with those words*.

It is very important to focus on what Jesus said next, "*you will ask what you desire.*" Notice the conditional progression of these verses: 1. *If* you abide in Me, 2. *And* My words abide in you, 3. You will ask what you desire. What is a conditional progression? The promise is conditional and progresses through "*if*" and "*and.*" The "*you will ask what you desire*" is predicated on the conditions stated by "*if*" and "*and.*" *If* you abide in Me, *and* My words abide in you. Those are the two conditions for asking what we desire. More importantly, they form the basis for our desire. *Our desires are created out of the vision God frames within us.*

> God created man from the creation
> to operate with Him in all He framed, formed, and filled.

When God frames the world, we are to create (in our understanding through a revelation of what He desires to create through us), He simultaneously creates a desire in us to create that world. The vision God frames in us also frames the desire to speak and release that vision into the earth. God is waiting to fulfill the desire of His heart through His partnership with the desire He places in our hearts. We do not ask out of self-generated desire based on what we see in the earth. We do not ask apart from abiding in Christ and His Word abiding in us. Our creative vision and desire must come from abiding in Christ and from His Word abiding in us. His Word is His will. Any other creative process equates to a self-generated vision apart from God; even if we claim to be doing it for and by Him with spiritual language while quoting scripture.

Because God gave dominion to man, He frames the world He desires to release into the earth in us by His Word so He can co-create with and through us into the sphere of our dominion and calling. We then speak to release and build the framework of the world God framed in us into the creation through and for Christ. Now, the world we framed can be formed as the fruit of abiding in Him and His Word abiding in us.

The second phase of God's creative process is *forming*. What is forming? It is when the creation responds to form what has been framed by the Word of God.

> In the beginning, God created the heavens and the earth.
> The earth was *without form and void*,
> and darkness was on the face of the deep.
> Genesis 1:1–2 (emphasis added)

What was the condition of the creation in the beginning? It was without form and void. God frames, then forms that which has no form. That is the next step in God's creative process. The creation narrative reveals this ongoing process. God spoke to frame the creation and the creation responded by taking on the form of what God spoke.

Open your Bible and read the creation narrative in Genesis. You will find, "then God said" throughout the verses. You will also find the created realm took the form of what God framed with His Word. For example, the waters and the dry ground were separated. That is a demonstration of the creation taking on the specific form of what God framed with His Word.

The third phase of God's creative process is *filling*. As you continue to read the creation narrative, you will find that God filled what He formed. He filled the air with birds, the land with trees, grass, herbs, the beast of the field and the waters with an abundance of living creatures. *God framed, formed and filled His creation.*

How did God create mankind? Through the same creative process He used to create the created realm; He framed, formed, and filled mankind. *"Then God said, Let us make man in our image, and according to Our likeness"* (Genesis 1:26). What did God do when He spoke those words? He *framed* the image of mankind. What did He do next? He *formed* him from the dust of the creation (Genesis 2:7). What did He do next? He breathed into his nostrils and *filled* him with the breath of life (Genesis 2:7). *God's creative process: He frames, forms and fills.*

God followed the same process when Christ came into the earth as the Last Adam. For millenia God released His prophetic word to frame the birth, life, death, and resurrection of the Messiah. God spoke His word through the prophets to frame the life and destiny of Christ. Then, when Holy Spirit overshadowed Mary with the seed from pre-fall Adam, God formed the Messiah in her womb to be born of a virgin just as the scriptures had framed it to be. Next, the Son of God left heaven and filled the form of man with the form of God. God's creative process: *He frames, forms, and fills*. God has not, and will not, change the process of creation He has made known to us.

God used the same process to create the created realm, to create mankind, and to bring His Son into the earth. We must follow the same process and pattern as God's co-creative disciples to bear much fruit. The coming of the Kingdom through the process of framing, forming, and filling is the process of merging heaven and earth.

There are some cases where we do not need to frame, form, and fill. We simply *release* what has already been framed, formed, and filled. Other times, we will frame and others will form and fill just like Paul said, "I planted, Appollos watered" (I Corinthians 3:6).

The flood in Genesis is a perfect example of releasing what has already been framed, formed, and filled. Genesis 7:11 says, *"on that day all the fountains of the great deep were broken up, and the windows of heaven were opened."* First, we notice that the earth and the fountains of the deep were already in place, and the windows of heavens were already

15 : OPERATING IN THE KINGDOM

in place. God had already framed and formed them, and in fact, He had already filled both the fountains of the great deep and the heavens.

What happened next? First, the fountains gave up their deep and then the heavens were opened. When the deep gives up what it has been filled with, the heavens open over that deep. What does this have to do with God's creative process? Everything. When the fountains of the deep were broken up and the heavens opened, God flooded the earth with the substance of the deep and the heavens. The heavens poured out what the fountains first released. The reality is, God baptized the earth in water and that is how He is going to fill the earth with the knowledge of the glory of the Lord, as well.

Habakkuk 2:14 says, "*For the earth will be filled with the knowledge of the glory of the Lord, as the waters cover the sea*" (emphasis added). Notice that the earth will be *filled* with the knowledge of the glory of the Lord. Not only does Habakkuk say the earth will be *filled*, he told us how it will be filled — *as the waters cover the sea*. I once asked the Lord, "How do waters cover the sea, when the sea is water?" He responded and said, "When it rains." Waters cover the sea when it rains. That is how the flood came and that is how the earth will be *filled* with the knowledge of the glory of the Lord.

> When God created man, He filled him with the breath of life.
> When we are born from above,
> God fills us with Himself to become our deep.

God caused the fountains to give up their deep and the heavens to open so the *earth* would be *filled*, not just the fountains and the heavens. When God created man, He filled him with the breath of life. When we are born from above, God fills us with Himself to become our deep. Jesus said, "*But the water that I shall give him will become in him a fountain of water springing up into everlasting life*" (John 4:14). In John 7, Jesus spoke about Holy Spirit in the believer, "He who believes in Me, as the scripture has said, out of his heart will flow rivers of living water. But this He spoke concerning the Spirit, whom those believing in Him would receive, for the Holy Spirit was not yet given because Jesus was not yet glorified."

What do we see here? We see that just like the fountains of the deep, God has deposited the waters in us by the indwelling of Holy Spirit. *We have already been framed, formed and filled*, so we need to *release* what we have been filled with to release the Kingdom on earth, as it is in heaven. Holy Spirit is in us and He searches all things, yes, the deep things of God to release them through us (1 Corinthians 2:10).

What do we have now? We have the same scenario as the flood. God has made us to be the fountains of the deep. We have already been framed, formed, and filled; now we need to release our deep. When we release our deep, the heavens release the exact same substance over us that we release into the earth, just like the flood. This time, God is releasing His Spirit to reveal His glory; He is releasing the hidden mystery of God in man. Our deep is the hidden mystery, the mystery that was ordained before the ages for our glory. Our destiny is to release the knowledge of that glory (of the Lord) as the waters cover the seas (1 Corinthians 2:7; Habakkuk 2:14).

When we release the deep within us through praise, prayer, worship, the prophetic, and by speaking the vision created by a revelation of Christ and His Kingdom, we create a sea of God's glory in this realm. The heavens then release the glory of God to rain upon the seas we have created to flood the earth with His glory.

> Operating in the Kingdom is a simple faith-based process: frame, form, fill, and release.

God is counting on us to operate in the Kingdom to co-create with Him, and to release what He has filled us with. We must be active "co-creators" and "glory releasers" with Christ. That is how God partners with us so it can be on earth as it is in heaven. Because we abide in Christ and He abides in us, we have access to the heavens in Christ and it gives Christ access to the earth through us. We have been given dominion and Christ desires to create worlds within this fallen world, with and through us, as we frame, form, and fill worlds within this world through and for Him. He then desires to release His glory and His Kingdom into those worlds.

When we receive our vision in Christ for what He wants to do in the earth, He frames it in us first to create that world. That world literally exists within us. The world He framed and created in us becomes our vision, our passion, and our God-given desire. God wants us to ask out of that desire so we can bear fruit as creative sons of our Father in heaven. We

15 : OPERATING IN THE KINGDOM

speak and release those words as decrees, declarations and proclamations to frame a world that will soon be formed in the created realm. How is that world formed in the created realm? In the same way that the created realm changed to form what God framed with His Word, the created realm will change to form what we have framed with His Word, released through manifest sons. The creation responds to the voice and presence of manifest sons.

The Lord once spoke to me and said, "Unrighteous men rape, pillage, and steal from the earth, but the earth willingly yields its treasures to the sons of God." How does that apply to forming the world we have framed with the Word of God? It means that things in the created realm will change to reflect who we are and what we say as sons of God. When we frame what God has spoken through us, the created realm is affected by those words. The worlds of finance, circumstance, government, relationship, and everything within our designated Kingdom domain will take on the form of what we framed. Jesus made it very clear,

> *If you abide in Me, and My Words abide in you, you will ask what you desire, and it shall be done for you. By this My Father is glorified, that you bear much fruit, so you will be My disciples.*
> John 15:7-8 (emphasis added)

When we abide in Christ, and His Words abide in us to create God's desire in us, what we ask and release will be done for us! The heavens will pour out all that is necessary to back the decrees and declarations we make with the word God gives us. When this happens, the creation responds to form the substance of what was framed by God's Word; all so it can be on earth as it is in heaven.

This begins with the understanding that we can see the Kingdom of God because we are born from above. What we see and hear there becomes the vision in our hearts that God desires to release into the earth through us. Once the world is framed and formed, then God fills that Kingdom environment with His own presence and that world then operates by Kingdom principles, not the principles of the world. Operating in the Kingdom is a simple faith-based process: frame, form, fill, and release.

CHAPTER 16: REDEMPTION AND THE COMING KINGDOM

Throughout this book, we have emphasized that God is merging five things: God and man, heaven and earth, time and eternity, the government of heaven and the governments of earth, and the communities of heaven and the communities of earth. We have emphasized what the fullness of redemption looks like for the believer and our responsibility to see into heaven to release it on earth as it is in heaven. We are the point of convergence for the redemption of those five areas. At this point, I want to speak about the merger of the government of heaven and the governments of earth.

The coming age has become the present age. It is no longer a matter of waiting; it is a matter of seeing, believing, and releasing a prophetic, intimate, and personal revelation of the person of Christ and His coming day. It is about God's government superseding man's government through sons who hear the voice of their Father in heaven.

God is longing to show us what He is going to do in the coming age, on *the day* when He establishes His eternal Kingdom on earth. He wants us to implement what we see to bring it into time now as an expression of our governing sonship and oneness with Christ. When we do, we will be laying the foundation for His eternal Kingdom government to land fully on earth as it is in heaven. God's government will bring the righteous and just nature of God Himself into the earth to be expressed through His sons in every area of life.

The church today is standing on the precipice between two ages: the church age and the age to come, the Kingdom age. We, like John the Baptist, are standing in one age while seeing, declaring, and releasing the next age. John preached, "Repent for the Kingdom of heaven is at hand." Then Jesus showed up and preached, "Repent for the Kingdom of heaven is at hand." John was a bridge between the old and the new, a bridge between the ages. John saw into the next age by the Spirit of God; he then became the gate through which the Kingdom arrived in the earth to prepare for Christ's arrival. John said the same thing Jesus was going to say when Jesus arrived, and so it is for us.

I have heard many describe this as a Joshua generation; I fully agree. But I also believe we have transitioned from a Joshua generation to a John the Baptist, or a 'bridge' generation. We are called to build and become a bridge between the ages like John the Baptist. As sons of our Father in heaven, we are called to transition the church from a self-focused church-age paradigm into an eternal Kingdom-age paradigm. It is a time of reformation. God is opening our eyes and our awareness to the fullness of restoration in Christ and our awareness of the heavens. He wants us to see what He is doing in heaven so we become the point of convergence to merge heaven and earth *before His return*. We do this by merging completely with Christ, His day, and all that is in Him to release His governing Sonship into the earth before His return.

What we are really talking about is an apostolic and prophetic reformation: an expression of heaven on earth through a revelation of the person of Christ, a release of the revelation God gave Jesus, and a revelation of His government the likes of which the world has never seen. Jesus was the first fruits of a reformation that is about to explode into the earth through apostles, prophets, kings and priests; through believers.

As we said in Chapter 11, when God created the Earth He used heaven as the template. When He created man, He used Himself as the template. When man fell, God and man and heaven and earth were separated. This reformation is the effectual reunification of all five areas we have discussed. What are really talking about? We are talking about God's thoughts and God's ways in heaven fully revealed and expressed through His relationship with redeemed mankind in the earth.

This reformation is not going to be a salvation move. It is not going to be a healing

16 : REDEMPTION AND THE COMING KINGDOM

move. It is not going to be a word move or a deliverance move. It is going to be a revelation of the person of Jesus Christ as King of kings, Lord of lords (which includes all the above), and a convergence of every move of God and Kingdom expression that has ever existed. It is going to merge God and man, heaven and earth, time and eternity, and heavenly and earthly governments. It will also merge the church in heaven with the church on earth; there is only one church and one body. You will see Jesus, the cloud of witnesses, and God's angelic army partnering with the church on earth to bring a level of unity and Kingdom awareness that will be staggering and unstoppable.

My friend Art Atkinson says, "Before God does a thing, He does a thing." In other words, the first fruit of a thing is an expression of the fullness of the thing that is coming. When you see a first fruit, know that a greater measure, a fullness of that first fruit expression, is coming. John the Baptist's message is an example of this very thing. God said "repent" through John; that is the first fruit. Then Jesus brought the fullness of that very same message.

Likewise, when Jesus was resurrected, graves were opened and many bodies of the saints who had fallen asleep were raised. He and those who were resurrected with Him walked around Jerusalem. That was God releasing a "first fruit resurrection" before the resurrection. But even beyond that, it was the first fruits of Jesus, the cloud of witnesses, and the church on earth walking the earth at the same time and working together. There were multiple generations in Christ working together, some who had died already — now resurrected with Christ — and others who were alive in Christ as a part of the church on earth, all walking and working together. Jesus and those resurrected in Jerusalem were the first fruits of Jesus and the cloud of witnesses working with us today, the present-day ecclesia.

This partnership allows those who have gone before us to once again engage in the fulfillment of their destiny and purpose to add their spiritual journey to our present-day journey. I have heard others refer to this generational partnership as the synergy of the ages. It will be the divine completion of God's plan to merge His Kingdom in heaven with the kingdoms of this world.

This all begins with a reformation of the apostolic and prophetic offices. It begins with the maturing of believers as they step into the realm of governing sonship and their roles as kings and priests. Let's talk about the apostolic and the prophetic reformation, the release of a new breed — *Kingdom apostles and prophets.*

What are Kingdom apostles and prophets? Kingdom apostles and prophets see into the coming eternal age and government of Christ (already present in the heavens) to implement here what they see Him doing there, and what they see Him doing in *His day*. This does not mean there have not been Kingdom apostles or prophets before. But the measure and reality of what God is releasing *now* is significantly greater than what He has released *before*. This release is hugely governmental, beyond the governmental authority assigned to the church. I have dubbed them *Kingdom* apostles and prophets based on the nature of their assignment *distinct and separate* from the church paradigm. They are given insight into the eternal day of Christ so they can lay the foundation for its full arrival, a foundation for God's Kingdom government to land on earth as it is in heaven.

The Lord recently made it very clear to me that He assigned the five-fold ministry of apostle, prophet, evangelist, pastor and teacher to the church, not the Kingdom. The church is a *part* of the Kingdom, not the *fullness* of the Kingdom. You cannot fit the ocean in a cup and you cannot fit the fullness of the Kingdom into the church. The five-fold ministry is church government and does not represent the full scope of kingdom government. Its purpose is two-fold: to govern the church and to mature the body of Christ until we reach the fullness of the measure of the stature of Christ (Ephesians 4:11-13). Sonship is the fullness of the measure of the stature of Christ; Jesus was the mature son of His Father in heaven (Matthew 3:17, 17:5).

When people mature into Kingdom sonship, they no longer need a tutor. They have a direct line of communication with their Father; by the Spirit, to be mentored beyond the realm of the five-fold. They are to be mentored by God, not man (1 John 2:27). That is where I believe we have made a huge mistake. The church continues to view those they have raised up to be under their management, but they are not. We cannot use "*covering*" as a means of control and a way to exercise continued authority over people who can hear from God for themselves. This practice is not pleasing to God.

As mature sons, believers are now under new management. They hear and see their

16 : REDEMPTION AND THE COMING KINGDOM

Father in heaven and administrate from their place in Christ. Sons hear the voice of their Father, not the voice of a religious or world system. God wants His sons released into the arena of their Kingdom purpose so the earth will be enveloped in a Kingdom environment, not merely a church environment. The Lord's Prayer is clearly on earth as it is in heaven, not on earth as it is in church. God's vision is bigger than the church. The church is a means to an end. God established and uses the church to mature believers so they can facilitate the coming of His Kingdom on earth as it is in heaven.

The current model trains up church workers to build a church and/or ministry. We are not called to build the church; Jesus said He would do that. Our assignment is to build people, not ministries. Our assignment is to build people, not programs. Our assignment is to train up and release sons into their Kingdom purpose; it is not to imprison them and their gifts in the local church to fulfill our vision or fill a vacancy in our ministry. As those who follow from the front, we should not ask believers what they can do for our ministry. We should be asking them what we can do to help launch them into their God-given purpose and destiny to change the world as we know it.

The five-fold ministry and Kingdom apostles and prophets have different assignments and purposes. As a result, those assigned to the church and those assigned to the Kingdom often struggle to understand each other. Why? The answer is very simple: because we have not understood that they have different purposes and different assignments. One assignment is not greater than the other, just different. That is why many apostolic and prophetic people have not fit into the church-paradigm very well. It is not their purpose or their assignment; the Kingdom and global governance are their calling. The Kingdom will never fit into the church, but the church does fit into the Kingdom. The Kingdom encompasses the church; the church does not encompass the Kingdom.

> If we get our roles confused, we will not understand our counterparts in their church or Kingdom assignments. A lack of understanding will bring a division rather than a partnership between those called to the church and those called to the Kingdom.

The five-fold (those assigned to the church) are called to allow Christ to govern the church through them based on a foundational revelation of Jesus Christ the head of the church; God administrates the church through them. They are also called to raise mature sons who know how to see and hear what our Father is doing in heaven the way Jesus did.

Kingdom apostles and prophets (those assigned to the Kingdom at this time in history) are called to establish and administrate God's Kingdom government on a foundational revelation of Jesus Christ the governing King. *God is going to administrate the nations through them.* If we get our roles confused, we will not understand our counterparts in their church or Kingdom assignments. A lack of understanding will bring division rather than a partnership between those called to the church and those called to the Kingdom. If for some reason, we find we cannot partner with our church or Kingdom counterparts, then we must learn to stay in our lane and let them be who God has called them to be. Do not criticize; we must stay in our lane and on task with our assignment.

Regardless of our assignment, we are a part of the church and the Kingdom. You may ask, "Can I be *assigned* to the church and the Kingdom?" Yes, you can be assigned to both. Paul is the perfect example of a person with an apostolic and prophetic calling assigned to both the church and the Kingdom. Paul was a huge part of laying the foundation of the church, but he was caught up into heaven and saw things that were unlawful for a man to utter (2 Corinthians 12:4). He saw both his current assignment in the church and the age to come. Many have the same assignment as Paul; they have been a part of the church-age and if they have eyes to see and ears to hear, they will function apostolically and prophetically to release the Kingdom-age as well.

When the Lord was unfolding this understanding to me He made one thing very clear. *Leaders who do not see this change coming cannot be leaders when it comes.* Why will they not be allowed to lead? Because they will lead from their experience in the old, rather than from God's vision of the new that He is releasing to those who have eyes to see and ears to hear. They will endeavor to put church boundaries and a local mindset around a global Kingdom assignment – *that will not work.*

God built the church on the foundation of the apostles and prophets with Jesus Christ as the chief cornerstone (Ephesians 2:20). He will build His Kingdom the same way. Isaiah said, "*I lay in Zion a foundation of stone, a tried stone, a precious cornerstone, a sure foundation*" (Isaiah 28:16). That is Mount Zion and Mount Zion is more than the church. It is the mountain of the Lord and it is the fullness of God's Kingdom and God's government (Hebrews 12:22-24).

When God established the church, He built it on the foundation of the apostles and prophets. The early church apostles and prophets had a revelation of Jesus as head of the church. Kingdom apostles and prophets have a revelation of Jesus the governing king and chief cornerstone of Mount Zion, the fullness of God's Kingdom and God's government. Scripture reveals two prototypes of Kingdom apostles and prophets; Daniel and John.

In Daniel 12:4, Daniel was shown a book and told to shut it up until the time of the end. Daniel saw the book; that is what prophets do, they see. In Revelation 10:8-9, John is shown the same book but told to eat it. Daniel saw the book and John ate the book. What is God saying by this? God buried His strategy for the coming age in the foundational gifts of apostle and prophet. Daniel and John stood in proxy for those called to see and release His Kingdom strategies in the time of the end. It has been hidden until now so the enemy could not counterfeit or preempt what God is about to do.

> The earth is going to change through the restoration of eternal purpose and generational inheritance, reaching as far back as Adam.

God is about to administrate the nations through these kingdom voices. He is going to give them open door entrance into heaven, into the heavens, and the multiple realms and dimensions in Christ to see His day and His strategies. Then, they will walk in the earth carrying what they received there, just like Peter carried what he received there and Paul revealed the "in Christ" realities he received there. They will receive divine favor to gain entrance into the offices of presidents, prime ministers, kings, princes, and all manner of earthly government. He is going to awaken the "little book" in them and they are going to share with leaders of local to global government what God is revealing for their region or nation. It does not mean every governmental leader will receive what is being released, but they will hear it and be held accountable for what has been shared with them. It will be their opportunity to partner with Christ and the coming of His Kingdom.

Furthermore, God is releasing a global jubilee. There is a time coming when you will see borders realign, or disappear, to reflect how God sees the nations, not how man has established them. The earth is going to change through the restoration of eternal purpose and generational inheritance reaching as far back as Adam. Remember what Paul said in his speech on Mars Hill? *"And He has made from one blood every nation of men to dwell on all the face of the earth and has determined their pre-appointed times and the boundaries of their dwellings"* (Acts 17:24-26; emphasis added).

Paul not only said God made from one blood every nation of men to dwell on all the face of the earth, he also said God determined their pre-appointed times and the boundaries of their dwellings. Man, through violence and the shedding of blood, has built kingdom after kingdom and stolen lands and tribal kingdom-based inheritances from their rightful heirs. God is going to rearrange the boundaries of national dwellings to restore generational blood-based inheritance so they are aligned with His heart and intent for the destinies of those people groups. He will restore the generational inheritance of every tribe and tongue.

Our role in the release of redemption and the coming age is simple; we are to be and function like Jesus. Jesus is in heaven with and in His Father. We are in heaven in Christ Jesus. We are in Christ, who is in the Father and we are filled with Holy Spirit. That is how and where we get our vision and our voice. While it appears we see dimly now, God is releasing great grace upon His church, upon His ecclesia, to live and see into the heavens within Christ with great clarity. Holy Spirit is going to show us things to come. What we *see there, decree there,* and *release there* will frame, form and fill us with God's vision for the earth, to bring the fullness of His Kingdom and His government to earth. The coming age has arrived and it is our responsibility to release its foundation so the fullness of heaven can land on it.

16 : REDEMPTION AND THE COMING KINGDOM

EPILOGUE

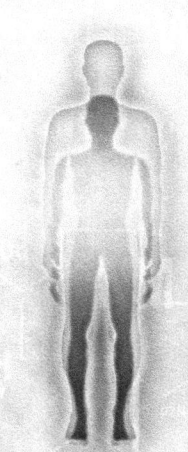

    Considering all that we have learned in the previous chapters, I am sure what I've written is a paradigm shift for many; a big picture that is almost unsettling. But that is okay; it was a major shift for me when God opened these truths to me over the course of several years. I live a lifestyle of constant inquiry. I practice the presence of God; always seeking, always asking God to reveal Himself to me through "revelationship." The things I've learned were built in me line upon line, and precept upon precept over the course of many years. The revealing of one truth led to another. Deep calls to deep (Psalm 42:7). The deeper I moved in understanding, the deeper the understanding that came my way; deep called to deep. It took time for deep to call to deep. But once I developed a deep, I had a deep to call another deep into my life.

    I wrote this book because I was encouraged to do so by my wife Laura, Dr. Ogbonnaya and some of our friends. Their encouragement was confirmed to me by an ongoing prompting from the Lord. As I wrote, He brought daily insight and clarity beyond what I knew when I started the book. What you have read is not merely information. Everything you have read is an expression of my life and relationship with God. I am sharing the results of 25 years of prayer, study, and revelationship with you.

    I want to be the living expression of what God reveals to me. It is my hope that you will become a living expression of what the Lord revealed to you through this book.

If you find you are not satisfied with where you are in your relationship with the Lord, that is a prompting and call to deeper things. At this point, your primary role is to seek God for yourself and ask Him what path you are to walk. Ask Him what systems of thought you currently hold need to be abandoned, and what thoughts and ways of believing you should keep.

If you are a pastor or a minister, I ask you to examine your motives. Do you have a personal agenda rather than a Kingdom agenda? Examine your life, your ministry, your motives, and your methods. Ask yourself if you are an expression of your denomination or an expression of God and His Kingdom. Are you an expression of a religious system or the expression of God and His Kingdom? Do you operate in fear of what man thinks or in awe of the Lord? I am asking this of you because I asked it of myself first.

I was a senior pastor for ten years and I am known as a revelatory Bible teacher. As the Lord revealed some of the truths in this book to me, I was nervous. It frightened me. How did it frighten me? The fear of man. Every time the Lord showed me something that did not line up with the doctrinal views I had been taught by others, I thought, "There goes my reputation" or, "What will so-and-so think if they find out I believe or teach this?" Ultimately, I reached a place of intimacy and hunger for the truth that overrode my fear of what man would think of this book. If I had not dealt with my fear of what man thinks, I would not have released this book. This book is a willful demonstration of my partnership with God in faith. Once this book is out, there is no turning back, I will be known by what I have written here.

What insight brought the most apprehension for me, the greatest fear? When the Lord told me He brought the seed from pre-fall, pre-sin, Adam. I have never heard anyone say that. But I must also tell you, the revelation that brought the greatest fear of man also brought the greatest understanding of the full restoration of man *including* the human genome. That single insight, that single key to the kingdom, unlocked a world of revelation that answered so many questions for me. It was a deep well that became the theme of this book.

Ask God about your current doctrinal positions and if they are the reason you are where

EPILOGUE

you are in your understanding and relationship with Him. In fact, I can tell you that you are where you are because of what you believe. If you do not agree with this book in its entirety, then take what you can receive from it and grow by it. One word, one understanding, or one thought from God can change your entire world. It cannot be overstated; our lives are the result of what we think. "As a man thinks in his heart, so is he" (Proverbs 23:7). "Be not conformed to this world, but be transformed by the renewing of your mind, that you may prove the good, acceptable, and perfect will of God" (Romans 12:2).

God is not keeping truth from us. He told us repeatedly throughout the scriptures how we think determines the course of our lives. That is why He has made His thoughts and His ways available to us. He wants us to think His thoughts. Why does how and what we think matter? Because Jesus said, "For out of the abundance of the heart, the mouth speaks" (Matthew 12:34). We end up saying what we think; what we say frames our world.

I have made a conscious decision to take thoughts captive and to bring them into obedience to Christ (2 Corinthians 10:5). As we said in Chapter 9, it is a part of overcoming to reign. I choose to engage in relationship with the Lord, with the Word, with Holy Spirit, and with everything heaven offers. One premise of this book is that God is merging five things: God and man, the heavens and the earth, time and eternity, the government of heaven and the governments of earth, and the communities of heaven and the communities of earth. We must understand that we are the focal point and primary mechanism of this merger. God is going to merge these areas through us as we are transformed through spiritual growth *and* the genetic redemption of our bodies. The more we are conformed to His image, the more heavenly Kingdom substance He can release through us.

I willfully think in accordance with God's Word, and I willfully speak to frame my world with what God has revealed to me. Why? So I can participate and be involved in the coming of God's Kingdom on earth as it is in heaven. The part of the Kingdom He reveals to me is the part of the Kingdom He wants to reveal through me. The part of the Kingdom He reveals to you is the part of the Kingdom He wants to reveal through you. He will use me, He will use you, and He will use us to frame, form, fill, and release worlds within worlds. Through our participation with that process, we become a Kingdom focal point and the mechanism to bring all God and heaven has to offer into the earth. Our hearts, our thoughts, and our words make us individual and corporate gateways through which the

Kingdom of God manifests in the earth.

I do not claim to have good, let alone, great science. I do not claim to have perfect theology. What I do claim, however, is a heart that seeks after God and wants to know the truth so that I, and others, can be set free by it.

Below you will find some steps I take to engage for the transformation of my life and the coming of God's Kingdom. It is by no means a complete list of my prayer life. This list should not become a set of principles or a to-do list apart from relationship with God. I do these things in relationship with God, and not as a matter of self-imposed law. I did not make this list as something to do; I made the list out of what I am already doing in my relationship with God. I do not do everything on the list every day. As I come to the Lord in prayer, and Holy Spirit prompts me, I engage one or more things on the list at His leading. One day I may only do one thing and I do it for a long time. Another day, I may not engage at all. Another day, I may engage several items several times a day. I engage as I am led. Do not let this list become something you do without heart engagement or intentional purpose. Lastly, when you engage: ask, seek, and knock, and know what you are engaging for.

1. I engage in prayer. I tell God I am willing and desire to be used in the merger of all things separated at the fall. I ask Him to make me a point of convergence so all that heaven offers flows into the earth through me. I speak out my desire.

2. I pray the Lord's Prayer with conviction and sincerity.

3. I receive communion. When I do, I engage the living genetic contract within it to bring about the full restoration of my life and the transformation of my very DNA. I break my genetic relationship with the record of sin and death and the body of sin that has been done away with. I ask the blood of Jesus to speak better things into my life than the blood of Abel.

4. I speak to my body. I tell my body that the law of the Spirit of the life in Christ has made me free from the law of sin and death. I tell my body that the body of sin has been done away with and that sin does not have dominion over me.

EPILOGUE

I tell my body that I am the body of Christ, not the body of the first Adam, but the resurrected body of Christ — the Last Adam. We are the body of Christ.

5. I pray in the Spirit (in tongues) to release mysteries and to engage in the process of overcoming to reign.

6. I ask the Lord to help me break any dependence I have on the kingdoms of this world so I may fully rely on and engage His Kingdom.

7. I draw on the finished work of Christ for the transformation of my body, my life, and my environment. I am not waiting on the return of Christ for the fullness of redemption any more than I am waiting on the return of Christ to be born from above.

As you engage the areas addressed in this book, you will discover the process of overcoming to reign may bring significant emotions, desires, and arguments to the surface. As I said in Chapter 9, if you are not careful, you may be tempted to engage in the activities brought to the surface when they are exposed by God's Word and His Spirit working in you. The process will engage your spirit, your soul, and your body to bring about your full transformation into sonship. As a result, it will expose what is in each of those areas. You may feel unsettled, restless, even agitated. You may be tempted in areas you have not been tempted in for years.

These areas are being revealed to you so you can overcome in that area of your life; do not fall victim to what is exposed when you seek the Lord for your transformation. You must face what is leaving your life; that can be unpleasant. You cannot conquer what you do not face. You will most likely discover things about yourself you are not comfortable with, things you do not like. Remain steadfast, pray in the Spirit, engage the blood of Jesus and do not give the emotions, thoughts, or desires your ongoing attention or energy. You become what you stare at; do not stare at or feed the things that are exposed in your life. *They are illuminated to be eliminated.* Face them, acknowledge them, and eliminate them by looking unto Jesus, the author and finisher of your faith.

Now, I bless you in the name of Jesus and ask that His full image, likeness, and Kingdom be expressed through your life. May He use you to reveal His Kingdom and His ways to people and the creation. I will close with a paragraph from the introduction.

"With that said, I must admit that I feel like I live in a place of ongoing illuminated ignorance. I think we have all heard it said, 'The more we come to know, the more we realize how much we do not know.' We can never claim to know it all, or that we have reached the pinnacle of understanding. No matter how much we think we know God and have things figured out, we have not scratched the surface of who God is *and who He created us to be.* We love God and want to please Him, but our view of Him is so limited. That is the case with me, and I am sure with you as well. The key is to keep moving forward on this journey, with the anointing that teaches us, into the full expression of who God has created and recreated us to be in and through Christ."

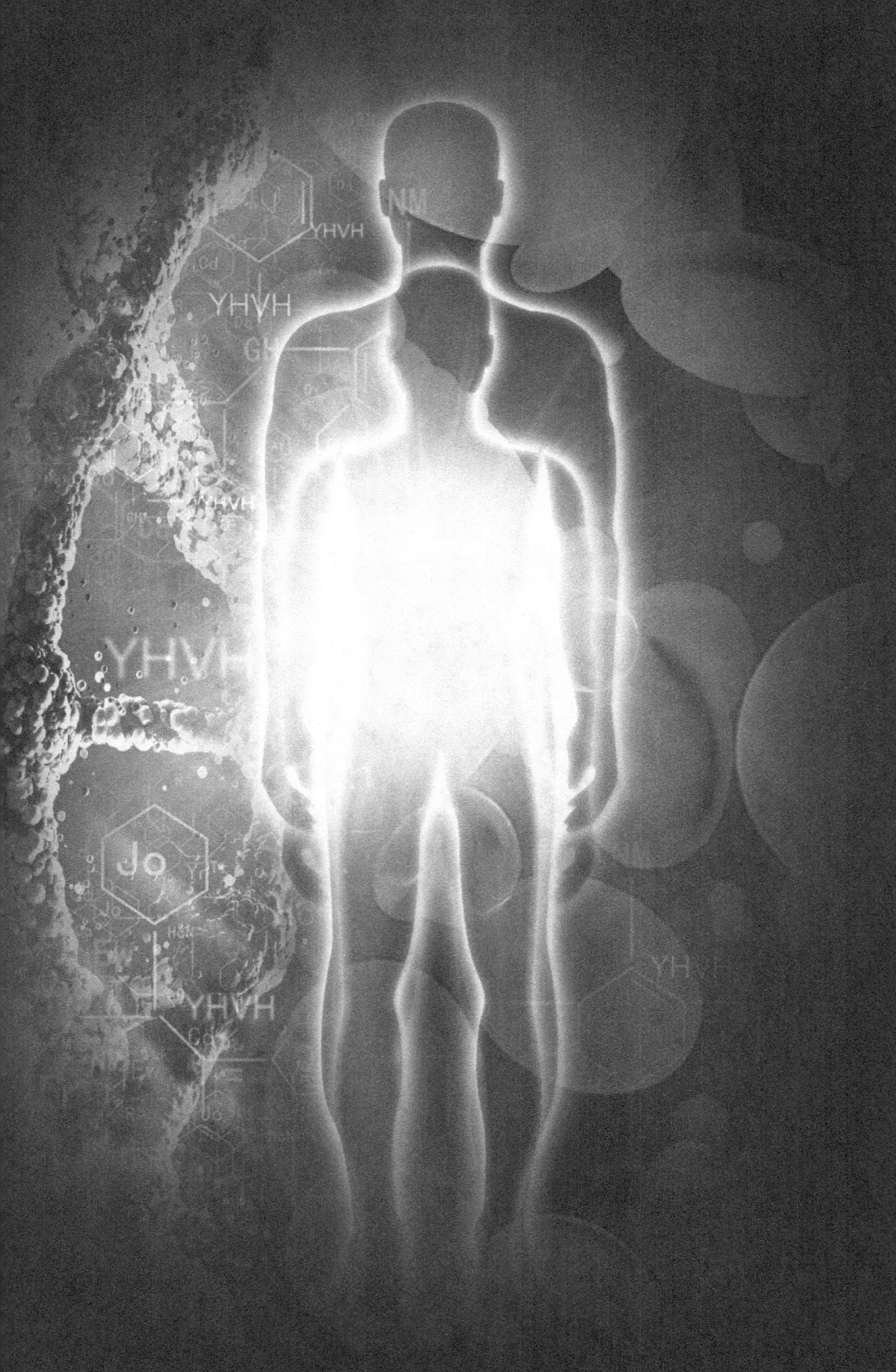

CONTACT INFORMATION

You can email us at: contact@redemptiveregeneration.com
Please visit our webpage at: www.redemptiveregeneration.com,
and our Facebook page at www.facebook.com/redemptiveregeneration

Heaven's Heart for Earth

Seraph Creative is a collective of artists, writers, theologians & illustrators who desire to see the body of Christ grow into full maturity, walking in their inheritance as Sons Of God on the Earth.

Sign up to our newsletter to know about the release of new books by Ron Jones as well as other exciting releases.

Visit our website :

www.seraphcreative.org

www.ingramcontent.com/pod-product-compliance
Lightning Source LLC
Chambersburg PA
CBHW051356290426
44108CB00015B/2034